THE BOBBS-MERRILL STUDIES IN SOCIOLOGY

The Dynamics of Industrial Society

Richard A. Peterson

THE BOBBS-MERRILL COMPANY, INC.
INDIANAPOLIS · NEW YORK

Library of Congress Cataloging in Publication Data
Peterson, Richard A.
The dynamics of industrial society.
(The Bobbs-Merrill studies in sociology)
Bibliography: p.
1. Industry—Social aspects. 2. Social change.
3. Organization. I. Title.
HD6955.P48   301.24'3   73-10094
ISBN 0-672-61324-7 (pbk.)

The Dynamics of Industrial Society

Introduction

1: The Classical Interest in Industrializing Society
Classical Economics
Classical Sociology
Changing Foci of Industrial Sociology

2: Industrializing Community: Institutions and Stratification
The Lynds in Middletown
Eclipse of Community
Quest for Community

3: Factory Studies: Productivity and Coordination
Orientation
Problems of Productivity
Problems of Organizational Coordination

4: Industrializing Society
Comparative Perspectives
Emerging Perspectives
The Industrial Sociology Yet to Come

References, Suggested Readings

This work is dedicated to the ones that will inherit the future: Michael, David, and Ruth. Special thanks go to Paul DiMaggio, Ernest Q. Campbell, Gerald Marwell, Claire L. Peterson, James D. Thompson, and Marcello Truzzi for their help in putting this work together. Marilynn Bennett, Naomi Smull, Trudy Masic, and Charlene Kirtley deserve much of the credit for their efforts in rendering this and other recent manuscripts into presentable form.

Since its beginning in the eighteenth century, the industrial revolution has affected every facet of Western society from work roles to religion. What is more, each new stage of industrialism has emerged before earlier stages have been completely absorbed so that society is in continual ferment. Thus America and the other "industrial" nations are nearly as "backward" as are the "developing" nations of Asia, Africa, and Latin America. We will focus on the dynamics of this process from a sociological perspective by focusing primarily on the consequences of industrialization.

Introduction

Over the past two centuries many proposals have been made for ways of dealing with the industrializing process. But the plans of priests, politicians, and paupers alike have met with very little success. Sociology and its sister discipline, economics, emerged in the late eighteenth century as part of this planning process. They were attempts to understand more scientifically the industrialization process, in hopes of bringing it more completely under human control. From Saint-Simon, Marx, and Spencer to Durkheim, Weber, and Ward, the founding fathers of sociology all focused their attention on industrialization and its consequences for society. Thus in this formative period of the discipline all of sociology was, in a sense, industrial sociology.

While most contemporary economists have concentrated on ever more abstract models of the factors of production, sociologists have tended to focus on the diverse "problems" which either derive from or are aggravated by industrialization. With the increasing specialization of sociology research in such diverse fields as urban social problems, stratification, family, revolution, the sociology of law, and the like, industrial sociology itself is often seen as just one more minor specialty area among many others.

Although it is often convenient to treat industrial sociology as a specialty in this way, we will organize and interpret the area more in line with its central place in the whole development of sociology. We will develop four themes which highlight the disruption, conflict, and reorganization of society deriving from the continuing process of industrialization:

1. the importance of industrialization in the formation of sociology
2. the continuing industrial revolution and its role in societal development around the world
3. industrialization in the community context

4. work roles and organization inside and outside the factory

Arranged in this order, the themes range from a long-term, large-scale concern with whole societies, to a short-term concern with small groups and individuals. Rather than discuss them in this order, however, the topics will be presented in order of their emergence as major foci of research in sociology—industrializing society, community, factory, then society again. This ordering facilitates an understanding of the evolution of research interests in the field and the relationship between industrial sociology and the rest of the discipline.

1 The Classical Interest in Industrializing Societies

The attempt to understand and thus to improve society is an age-old quest. Medieval and early modern scholars, more or less freeing themselves from the idea that social order is subject to divine whim, identified the political domain as the most crucial determinant of the quality of life which might be brought under human control. This political focus was held by men with as otherwise diverse religious and cultural views as Thomas Aquinas (1225–1274), Niccolo Machiavelli (1469–1527), Thomas Hobbes (1588–1679), Charles Montesquieu (1689–1785) and Jean-Jacques Rousseau (1712–1778). This 500-year period saw the emergence of the nation-state and with it the spread of domestic tranquility throughout most of Western Europe. This pacification had a number of far reaching consequences. Insofar as families and towns did not have to stand in perpetual military preparedness against their nearest neighbors, they could turn to the pursuits of production and trade. Land, which in the feudal era had been valued for the men and horses it could support for the uses of war, now became valuable for the wealth it could produce. Regions which had been self-sufficient increasingly produced those crops which were most profitable, and depended on trade to provide other goods. Increased commerce led to demands that the government not only maintain domestic tranquility but provide better roads and harbors, insure a stable currency and banking system, establish a system of commercial law, and encourage economic development through diverse other means. At the same time there were strong counter-demands that the government protect the privileges of the nobility, church, and feudal guilds against the rising industrialists.

CLASSICAL ECONOMICS

The political theorists engaged in a lively argument about the nature of government and the rights of man, but gradually a new theory emerged which was rooted in the economic realities of emerging capitalism. This theory of "political economy" was given its first full expression in 1776 by Adam Smith in his famous *Wealth of Nations.* His main ideas are worth noting, because they lead so directly to those of the first sociologists. He asserted that the wealth of a nation depends not on the amount of its accumulated gold, then a prevalent theory, but on the economic productivity of its people, which in turn depends on the degree to which jobs are specialized—what he calls the *division of labor.* The division of labor increases productivity, Smith argued, because the greater the specialization of any one unit (person, firm, or geographic region), the more expert it is likely to become at its given task, the more likely it will invent improved methods of production, and the more it will rely on other specialized units to fill its other needs. In this cyclical process, the demand for production and commerce will become ever greater.

Smith's theory has clear political implications. Since the wealth of any nation depends on its productive capacity, any government restriction on the working of the free market, through tariffs or the protection of monopolies, reduces the aggregate national wealth by supporting less efficient producers. The mechanism which should control the level of production is the "unseen hand" of the perfectly competitive market. According to this theory the economic function of the government is to prevent the creation of private monopolies which are in restraint of free trade. These were a persistent danger even in 1776. As Smith observed, those persons "active in some trade seldom meet together but the conversation ends in a conspiracy against the public" (Smith, 1937:289). Beyond this, he argued that the government should provide the legal and monetary framework within which orderly economic activity could take place, thus encouraging business activity *in general* without favoring any segment *in particular.*

Smith was not insensitive to the negative consequences of the division of labor for the individual worker. As he notes:

> *The understandings of the greater part of men are necessarily formed by their ordinary employment. The man whose life is spent in performing a few simple operations . . . has no occasion to exert his understandings . . . he naturally loses therefore the habit of such exertion, and generally becomes as stupid and ignorant as it is possible for a human creature to become . . . his dexterity at his own particular trade seems, in this manner, to be acquired at the expense of his intellectual, social, and marital values. But in every improved and civilized society this is the state into which the laboring poor, the great body of the people necessarily fall, unless the government takes some pains to prevent it (Smith, 1937:734).*

While Smith did suggest that the government provide education to counteract the stultifying influences of the work place, he did not elaborate this idea or trace the further ramifications of the division of labor on other aspects of the society at large.

Other economists did not take up the task because their theory which was dubbed the "dismal science" defined the deprivation, exploitation, and civil strife of the time as necessary byproducts of industrialization. From their theory they argued that all attempts at increasing social welfare were foredoomed to failure because they would only increase the level of poverty or the number of the poor. They predicted that feeding the unemployed would reduce their desire to work and feeding the starving would only increase the numbers of the poor free to propagate more of their kind.

But the great social events of the times caught up with these theorists. The increasing level of industrial turmoil in England, as well as the bloodletting and ferocity of the French revolution—fueled by worker discontent and led by the emerging business classes against the preindustrial economic interests—led many scholars to question the laissez-faire stance of classical economics. Conservative scholars decried industrialization. They urged the government to prohibit the introduction of machinery and argued for the revitalization of the medieval craft guilds.

CLASSICAL SOCIOLOGY

In contrast to these pessimists, a number of scholars began to study the social consequences of the industrial revolution in hopes of being able to speed its development while mitigating its negative consequences. Their optimism was based on the idea that by using reason and applying the methods of science to social affairs, man could come to understand, and thus control, societal evolution. This was the basic ambience of the founding fathers of sociology, Comte Henri de Saint-Simon (1760–1825), Auguste Comte (1798–1857), Karl Marx (1818–1883), and Herbert Spencer (1820–1903).[1]

While they did not agree on what particular social policy should be followed, they shared a common perspective which can be stated briefly: Society is a system of interdependent parts which is evolving from an undifferentiated primitive communalism toward an ever more structurally differentiated civilization. Thus, in effect, the earlier sociologists took Adam Smith's ideas about the increasing division of labor and generalized it to all aspects of society. In doing so, they borrowed heavily from emerging theories of biological evolution which accented the struggle for resources and the survival of the fittest. Given this theoretical perspective, none of the early sociologists saw societal evolution as a tranquil or orderly process. But they heralded the Industrial Revolution, in spite of its many disruptive consequences for other aspects of society, because its greater differentiation and specialization of activities signaled a higher stage of societal evolution.

Tradition to reason The sociologists saw a new habit of thought called "positivism" by Comte to be central in the industrializing process. Briefly stated, it involved the substitution of calculation for tradition, and sociologists saw this change taking place in all aspects of social life. In the marketplace prices were increasingly set by the mechanisms of supply and demand rather than by custom. Scientific methods of inquiry and experimentation were replacing habitual methods of manufacture. Democratic competition was replacing established authority in politics, and rationalism was challenging religious dogmas.

1. Rather than cite all the relevant writings of the men discussed in this section, the reader is referred to Don Martindale (1960), Robert Nisbet (1966), and Irving Zeitlin (1968) for three quite different points of departure in understanding the early development of sociology.

As a consequence of these changes, Henry Sumner Main argued human social relations were increasingly governed by what he termed "contract" rather than by "status." That is, people increasingly regulate their reciprocal obligations rather than rely on traditional fixed conventions for guiding their behavior. Thus, for example, the peasant who owed the lord a fixed number of days of work per year in exchange for fixed rights to the land, was being replaced by wage workers who negotiated a cash wage in exchange for factory work. Looking at these same developments, Charles Cooley noted that "primary" social relationships, such as those in a family which bind people together in a broad range of relationships, were inceasingly being augmented by "secondary" relations, in which people interact with many others who are for the most part strangers. Generalizing this idea about the consequences of the division of labor, Ferdinand Tonnies contrasted the close-knit preindustrial community with the more highly differentiated postindustrial society.

Alienation and solidarity Many scholars were alarmed about the weakening of traditional values and conventional religion in the new industrial age of "reason." Comte argued that the increasing division of labor would "disperse" sentiment so that no one would feel strong loyalties or commitments to others. Fearing this tendency, he offered sociologists as a priesthood for a new religion based on reason.

It was not until sixty years after this empty offer that Emile Durkheim published in 1893 the closely argued theory that the division of labor not only alienates people from each other as Smith and Comte feared, but that it can also be the *basis* of a different form of solidarity. He asserted that preindustrial societies had been held together "mechanically" by common kinship, political, and religious loyalties, but that the various units of the highly differentiated industrial society are held together "organically" by their mutual interdependence.

Power The most conspicuous consequence of industrialization to engage the interest of early sociologists was the shifting focus of power in society. Herbert Spencer, for example, asserted that preindustrial Western society. had been controlled by a coalition of the landed aristocracy, the established church, and the royal government. This he termed "military society." The emerging industrial society, he argued, would be more devoted to commerce than to war. Its structure therefore would be influenced more by economics and commercial interests than by those of traditional politics and religion. Thus, it would be free of war. Reviewing the same historical record, Karl Marx asserted that during *each* era the owners of the economic resources, whether capitalists, feudal lords, or slave masters, have been able to create a political, military, legal, and religious system which bolsters and sanctifies their economic dominance. According to Marx's interpretation, each successive dominant economic interest has been overthrown by the classes it exploited. The catastrophic wars of this century mock Spencer's prediction of peace-with-industralization, and few social scientists now read Spencer. Even though the kind of proletarian revolution Marx predicted well over one hundred years ago has nowhere occurred, his theory of exploitation has energized more sociological research than any other body of ideas.

CHANGING FOCI OF INDUSTRIAL SOCIOLOGY

The *speculative* era of sociology drew to a close about 1920, but the ideas developed in that area have been the basis for the *empirical* research of most sociologists for the half-century since. While research in the industrial area has been quite diverse, most of it can be understood in terms of six major questions which derive directly from the concerns of the classical era:
1. What are the effects of industrialization on the various institutions of society?
2. What are the effects of industrialization on the stratification of society?
3. Why do men work and when do they revolt against work?
4. What are the most efficient forms of industrial organization?
5. What are the factors which shape the evolution of industrial society?
6. What effect does industrialization have on social problems?

Research has not focused equally on all six of these questions at any one time. Rather, each question has received more or less attention in turn. The first two, which concern the impact of industrialization on other aspects of the community, predominated in the 1920s and 1930s. For the sake of brevity this orientation will be called the *industrial community* approach. The second pair of questions, focusing on work and work organizations, emerged in the 1930s and held the greatest amount of research interest in the following two decades. It may conveniently be called the *factory* approach to industrial sociology. The final orientation, which has received ever increasing attention since 1955, focuses on the last two questions posed above. This *industrializing society* approach puts the problems of industrialization into the broader concern with societal modernization both in advanced nations and in the rest of the countries around the world.

Before exploring the three major foci just identified, two final introductory caveats need to be made. First, we are making a broad definition of the scope of industrial sociology, including many research works which deal with the diagnosis of industrialization even though they were not written by men identified as industrial sociologists or written as works in industrial sociology. Only the "factory" section falls within the purview of what is narrowly defined as industrial sociology. Second, in this short work, we can make no complete survey of all available research. Instead, the classical works will be stressed as much as the most recent findings, for, while now dated and obsolete in descriptive detail, the early works often most clearly define the intellectual problems and set the framework for the research that followed.

2 Industrializing Community: Institutions and Stratification

With a few notable exceptions, the work of the classical period of sociology was speculative in nature. When, after World War I, sociologists turned to testing theory by gathering data, they encountered great difficulty, as most theories concerned the dynamics of entire societies over long periods of time. One of the most successful techniques of reducing research to a manageable scope was to substitute for the entire society the intensive study of a single representative community. Researchers in this tradition, which flourished during the 1920s and 1930s and has continued up to the present, seek out communities that will represent the society at large or at least one of its important segments. They use the ethnographic method to describe and show the relations among all elements of the community. The best of these also research enough of the development of the community to provide not only a portrait of one point in time but also a moving picture of the dynamics of change over time.

This community focus is best suited to researching the first two of the six questions posed above, those having to do with the relationship of industrialization to (1) the institutional order, and (2) social stratification. These studies employ a system perspective. They show the ways in which changes in technology, factory production, work roles, and corporate organization have affected the family, politics, education, religion, and relationships between social classes. They also show how changes in these spheres have influenced the development of industrialization.

THE LYNDS IN MIDDLETOWN

In the sections which follow, we will make extensive use of the single most comprehensive study of an industrializing community, that made by Robert and Helen Lynd of Muncie, Indiana. Their first report, *Middletown,* compares the mid-1920s, a time of economic prosperity, with 1890 when Middletown, a rural county seat, was first being industrialized following the discovery of an abundance of natural gas in the vicinity four years earlier. A second book, *Middletown in Transition,* was researched during the acute depression years of the mid-1930s. Taken together, the studies provide an excellent picture of the ways that the various institutions of the community contribute to industrialization and how the introduction of new technologies continually disturbed the institutions of a representative American community over half a century.

While Middletown is ethnically homogeneous, having more native born residents and fewer Blacks, Jews and Catholics than most small industrial cities, it is not without cleavages. As the Lynds note, it is the "division into working class and business class that constitutes the outstanding cleavage in Middletown. The mere fact of being born upon one or the other side of the watershed roughly formed by these two groups is the most significant single factor tending to influence what one does all day long throughout one's life; whom one marries; . . . and so on indefinitely throughout the daily comings and goings of a Middletown man, woman, or child" (Lynd and Lynd, 1929: 23–24).

Craft factory to mass production   Changes in the working class segment of the community between 1890 and 1925, resulting from changes in the modes of factory production, were most conspicuous, so they will be discussed first. During this time the leading mode of factory technology changed from *craft-factory* to *assembly-line mass production*. The production of glass bottles, a leading industry in the community since the gas boom, illustrates the changes in the mode of production quite clearly. In the former technology, master craftsmen performed tasks requiring great skills, using large but simple machines and aided by a number of less-skilled artisans and apprentices. Through learning by helping, all of these aspired to become master craftsmen—members of the highly paid, powerful, and respected elite of the working class.

Spurred by the success of Henry Ford in using mass production techniques in building automobiles, the system of glass jar production underwent profound changes by the mid-1920s. System engineers analyzed the glass-blower's art, separated the components into simple routines and designed jar-making machines requiring workers with little skill to operate. As one glass blower commented plaintively in 1924, "You can take a boy fresh from the farm and in three days he can manage a machine as well as I can, and I've been at it 27 years" (Lynd and Lynd, 1929:74). By 1925, such assembly-line mass production machines had completely replaced the older mode of production in glass and most other factories, including the several auto parts plants which had come to Middletown.

The assembly-line production destroyed the craft skill hierarchy of workers in which there had been an association between age, skill, and pay. Mass production technologies put an accent on manual dexterity and docility, and in the absence of labor unions to enforce a norm of seniority, younger female workers were preferred to older males. Thus, even in the relatively high employment years of the 1920s, male heads of household often were laid off of their jobs while their wives and daughters were able to find employment. These changes in technology and employment had far-reaching effects on worker morale which we will discuss below. Here we will focus on the concomitant changes in the life outside the work place.

Working class schools   Assembly-line production finally broke the age-old custom of fathers passing skills on to their sons. Parents increasingly pressed their children to go to school, often making great personal sacrifices so that their children could eventually get "better" white collar and professional jobs. While it is true that the school system has operated as a great channel of intergenerational mobility, the public school system has not afforded equal opportunity to all. As the Lynds and hundreds of more recent studies have shown, the children of workers have been shunted into vocational rather than academic programs or shamed out of school by their business class peers, because they could not participate in the extracurricular social life of clubs and sororities surrounding the school. Thus, in effect, the schools have operated in such a way as to sustain the *belief* in equal opportunity while most often shunting children along social class lines roughly parallel to those of their parents.

For most children, schools in working class neighborhoods have taught the rudimentary skills necessary for adjustment to assembly-line factory work. The willingness to follow arbitrary orders, the rudiments of reading and arithmetic necessary to shop routines, the ability to persevere through a dull routine, and the values of patriotism and free enterprise were inculcated so that the worker would reject any person or idea labelled as foreign or anticapitalist. In the extreme cases, Berg (1971) has recently argued that the school has become a holding-tank which keeps children off the streets and off the job market for ten years while imparting little useful knowledge.

The one area of school life that the Lynds found received wholehearted community support was athletics. Begun in the 1880s as a means of instilling discipline, health, and physical fitness in all children, varsity athletics had become a major form of adult entertainment and civic pride. By the 1920s, high school sports rivaled religion as a symbol of community solidarity, as a teacher of morals (loyalty, self-sacrifice, fair play), and as a diversion from the harsh and drab realities of the work-day life.

Working class values   Karl Marx long ago identified religion as an "opiate" of the workers, in that it indoctrinated them into a numb, uncritical acceptance of the status quo. Certainly many of the beliefs and practices of the working-class oriented churches of Middletown were found by the Lynds to have this characteristic. The churches taught that life is brutal and short— a testing ground for a future life—that poverty is a virtue, life predestined, and individual salvation the goal. Spiritualist ministers offered to heal the sick, restore eyesight, and communicate with the dead. Working class ministers sometimes spoke out against union organizations and Roosevelt's New Deal. More often, they avoided current social issues and concentrated on themes of fatalistic acceptance of life as it is.

Other scholars have studied the uses of the working class church more thoroughly than did the Lynds. Pope (1965), in a study of North Carolina textile mills, found that mill-town preachers were paid by mill managers to inform on potential agitators among the workers. In like manner, the Salvation Army was supported by business interests in the Pacific Northwest to counter the organizing efforts of the International Workers of the World before the First World War, while in the same era, the Young Men's Christian Association was used to channel the "excess energies" of young workers into athletic pursuits. The YMCA and various temperance leagues worked against the use of alcohol and solicited the backing of business class interests by promising to maintain worker sobriety and docility (Gusfield, 1963).

Working class community The Lynds found little change in the nature of formal religion between 1890 and 1935 except for a greater segregation of churches along class lines. In sharp contrast, working class politics and leisure as well as their communal life generally had undergone great change. In 1890 the craft unions, which were composed of all workers in the same trade irrespective of their employer, exercised great influence in regulating the conditions of work, policing seniority rights of their members, and overseeing apprenticeship training in the factory. Beyond the factory, the craft unions also formed the hub of the working class community's life. They were the prime channels through which workers expressed political influence. Jointly, they engaged in patriotic celebrations, sponsored sports contests, invited nationally known union and political leaders to speak on a wide range of subjects, and carried on a wide range of cultural programs including a lending library containing many books on science, economics, and public affairs to broaden the intellectual life of members and their families. In addition, the unions built large accident and death benefit funds for their members. Thus, in the days *before* government-supported welfare programs, the craft unions looked after their own from cradle to grave.

A vestige of this craft union-based system of working class communities survived up to the 1950s in industries which retained their craft base of technology such as printing (Lipset, Trow, and Coleman, 1956; Blauner, 1964) but the system dissolved with the substitution of mass production for craft production. This had already taken place by 1924 when the Lynds reached Middletown. They found working class life in a state of flux and only just beginning to be organized along the quite different lines we know today. These changes can be seen in the areas of union organization, charity, and politics.

Industrial labor unions which group together all those in one factory and industry irrespective of their type of work, such as the United Auto Workers and United Steel Workers, were just being formed when the Lynds were making their second study. Since World War II such industrial unions have brought much more stability to mass production employment by winning seniority and other job rights from reluctant employers. "Charity," much in demand given the periodic unemployment of the 1920s and the Great Depression of the next decade, was administered by a complex of religious and city government agencies. The federally supported programs of accident insurance, unemployment compensation, social security, homeowners' insurance, and medicare, which today protect working class families against many financial disasters, had not yet been enacted.

Working class political interests, which in the 1890s had been expressed through the craft labor guilds, found expression through the ward bosses of the two major parties in most large cities by the 1920s. The politics of most small cities like Middletown, however, were almost exclusively in the hands of business class interests. Control over the mass media was important in gaining class control. In 1890 local newspapers were sustained by selling copies to the public, therefore their prime interest was in printing anything which would be of interest to their readers. By 1925, however, newspaper profits depended almost entirely on the amount of local advertisements they received. After examining the Middletown papers of the two periods, the Lynds concluded, "Independence of editorial comment happens to be in rough inverse ratio to the amount of advertising carried. The leading paper rarely says anything editorially calculated to offend local business; the weaker paper takes a stand editorially from time to time on such safe matters as child labor" (Lynd and Lynd, 1929:475). The effect was that business class interests were reflected not only in the editorial columns but also in the selection of news and even advertising. For example, in 1924 the local Chamber of Commerce secured the agreement of each local newspaper *not* to print advertisements for high paying jobs available in other cities. In this way they could "protect" their low local wages and pool of employable workers.

Consumerism One of the most pervasive changes in the life of working and business class alike was the spread of consumerism (the substitution of store-bought for homemade) into all aspects of life. It is an integral part of the division of labor in that having the money necessary to purchase consumables depends on specialization, and specialization in turn requires a wider range of consumer purchases which in turn provides work in ever-more specialized activities, and so on. Consumerism has been augmented by the decisions of workers over the past century. As their real wages have risen, they have invested most of this gain in a higher standard of living rather than in shorter hours of work. While American workers' real wages have increased more than ten-fold since the Civil War, their average hours of employment have been cut by less than half.

Consumerism was not simply a welcome byproduct of mass production, it was an absolute necessity. As Henry Ford, one of the great innovators in mass production, realized, industry could afford the elaborate technology and engineering costs of the assembly line only with volume production. To this end, he reduced the cost of his famous Model T from $900 in 1909 to $360 in 1914. Ford's belief in the economics of mass production was vindicated and he was able to raise wages from $2.40 for a nine-hour day to $5.00 for an eight-hour day, thus "compensating" workers for the tedium of the assembly line work and forestalling union organization of his workers (Galbraith, 1967).

Consumerism was not only facilitated by higher wages, it was prodded by the new styles of advertising, which about the turn of the century shifted from drab accounts of a product's specifications to slick appeals to the emotions. Advertisers did not confine their efforts to pushing one or another particular product, rather consumerism was increasingly equated with patriotism. As a 1924 Middletown newspaper columnist wrote, "The American citizen's first importance to his country is no longer that of citizen but that of consumer. Consumption is a new necessity . . . the way to make business boom is to buy" (Lynd and Lynd, 1929:88).

Consumerism was greatly facilitated by the vast expansion of credit in the first decades of this century. The expansion of installment buying allowed workers to purchase "on time" items they could not afford out of savings. Such consumerism-induced indebtedness motivated workers to seek overtime pay, second jobs, and employment for their wives. This new income and credit-derived purchasing power has not only gone on into buying more or better products of traditional sorts, such as processed foods, ready-made clothes and the like, but has gone into newly invented items which themselves often open whole new realms of consumption.

Henry Ford's Model T was the singularly most important new item of this sort. The auto was advertised as making possible all sorts of family outings. In fact, its introduction had just the opposite effect. With it the father could drive farther to work—or more accurately move his family to a home farther from the plant. His new neighbors would not likely work at the same place, thus increasing the physical and social distance between family and job. Mothers could range farther in search of bargain consumer items, thus threatening the low-volume neighborhood store. Teenagers could use the auto to get further away from adult social control. And family members could get into the country on weekends rather than go to church. Not only did the auto broaden the scope of secondary as opposed to prime contacts (see page 10) but it also introduced a vast diversity of new consumption opportunities in its wake.

Domestic Economy   At the beginning of the industrial revolution, most of the few items a working class family consumed were produced by family members. Food, clothing, and shelter were all homemade. By 1890 this had begun to change, and by 1924 the home was a prime realm of consumerism. Houses were built by specialists, clothes were store-bought, and food was increasingly canned, processed, or otherwise fabricated for easy meal preparation. What is more, an increasing array of labor-saving appliances, such as electric stoves, refrigerators, vacuum cleaners, washing machines, and dishwashers, lightened the job of keeping house. Tasks which had consumed the full energies of the housewife plus older female relatives, paid servants, and children could, by 1924, be accomplished with less than the full efforts of one woman. Older female relatives, now just economic burdens, were relegated to county- or church-sponsored homes for the aged— the precursors of today's retirement communities.

Children who could no longer contribute to the family economy became instead prime foci of consumption. The evolving specialty of child psychology which was taught through women's magazines and home economic classes, demanded that women spend much more time, effort, and emotional energy in training their children. Since fathers could rarely pass their job skills on to their children, increasingly greater amounts of money had to be set aside for their education through high school, and college. As the Lynds (1929:23–127) note, in the space of little more than one generation, the norm of "having all the children that God will send" was rapidly replaced by a norm of two to four children, even though the means of contraception were crude and imperfect.

Women not only spent a greater amount of their energy in the conscious socialization of their children, as compared with earlier times, they were more involved in religious, civic, cultural, charitable, and recreational ladies clubs. While often lampooned in the press and cartoons, these club activities were quietly devoted to the emancipation of women from the legal and psychic mastery of their husbands and confinement in the home.

Coupled with the introduction of labor-saving appliances into the domestic economy, increased opportunity for gainful employment outside the home has served as the great emancipator of women. In 1900, fewer than one in six workers were female, but by the 1970s this ratio has risen to better than one in three, and an increasing proportion are married women who manage not only a job but a home. This tremendous demographic shift in employment can be traced primarily to two factors: the greater use of machines in factory production and the great expansion in office and service occupations, both of which have opened a vast number of jobs women are physically able to perform. The new labor-saving devices not only served to free women for jobs outside the home, but also forced many of them into gainful employment in order to help finance the ever-rising standards of labor-saving technology in the home.

In the Lynds' view, the realm of work had changed more than any other between 1890 and 1935, but the changes in the family seem almost as great. At the earlier date the family was the center of most activities, but during this century a number of specialized agencies have changed this. The home has been more completely segregated from the work place. From vocational education to new techniques of homemaking, the socialization of the young has become the province of professional educators. Care of the sick and aged has similarly been taken over by professional experts. Family-centered religious activities are almost completely a thing of the past, and in the area of leisure, the family outings have been replaced by numerous activities geared to the particular interests and energies of one or another age group. Since the Lynds wrote, these age groupings have evolved into generation-specific culture styles which in many ways are opposed to each other and thus have great potential social and political import.

Business class community Most of the trends just described affected the business class community as much as the working class. Several aspects of industrialization, however, affected the two classes rather differently. The first is the area of work itself. The second is the realm of values. In 1890 most Middletown residents, like their counterparts around the nation, were self-employed or worked in a family business. The only industrial occupations which required formal education were in the areas of engineering, law, and financial bookkeeping. The many young men who worked as secretaries and assistants did so in order to "learn the business" so that they could go into business for themselves. Their exchange of practical training for work was modeled on the age-old apprenticeship system. Many business class fathers, themselves self-made men, counseled their sons against too much formal education and saw college as a place where one was likely to do little more than indulge in the excesses of alcohol or religion.

But the organization of business was changing rapidly. By 1890 the leading businesses of the nation, such as railroads and steel companies, were expanded well beyond the size that could be managed by the age-old patrimonial system. Machines, technologies, laws, and marketing practices were changing so rapidly that traditional procedures were soon outmoded, and the traditions of the past were not always the best advice for the future.

The joint stock corporation was the social invention employed to amass the great amounts of capital necessary to finance the ever more expensive machinery of production. Bureaucracy, adapted from the military and railroads, was employed to coordinate the efforts of the ever more diverse army of workers, engineers, accountants, and salesmen in the industrial firm. The inner workings of bureaucracy will be discussed below; here we are interested in its effects on other institutions of the community.

In 1890 only the railroad and post office workers were employed by firms not headquartered in Middletown. The Lynds do not give exact figures for 1925 or 1935, but by that time all but one of the major employers were branch plants of corporations centered outside Middletown. For them, the community was simply the cheapest, or otherwise more convenient, place to produce products or components. They had little regard for the community life beyond the supply of willing workers, police and fire protection for the plants, and low tax rates. But it was not only in the area of manufacturing that absentee owners had taken control. Many of the family-run retail stores had been driven out of business or absorbed by the economically advantaged "chain" stores centered elsewhere.

As a consequence of these changes in ownership and control, the sons of the business class could not look forward to succeeding their fathers in business. Thus, just as in the case of the elder craftsmen of the working class, there were few specific skills that business class fathers could teach. Increasingly, their sons looked to high school, trade school, college, and professional school as a means of getting ahead in futures which took them outside of Middletown. As school became ever more crucial, great efforts were made to keep business class schools better than those for the working class, and an elaborate system of social clubs evolved to insure that students would associate with "those of their own kind." In effect, the business class home and school became early training grounds for learning the skills necessary for getting along in a national business class labor market.

Business class values   For the most part, the small business community acted as if its power and local autonomy had not diminished. Caught in its own propensity to advertise rather than analyze, it conducted "booster" campaigns through the Rotary, Dynamo Club, and Chamber of Commerce to promote local business and convince themselves that the world around them was not changing. Much of this effort was couched in terms derived directly from Protestant Ethic admonitions to hard work and individual responsibility for success or failure. Rather than attack corporate enterprise as a threat to classical free enterprise, the boosters attacked state and federal government encroacïment as well as the liberal ideas of clergymen, government officials, and college professors who were beyond their control. Not until the great economic and political upheavals of the Great Depression of the early 1930s did it become painfully obvious to the business class that their relatively autonomous community had been eclipsed by economic and social forces beyond their communal control.

Changing stratification   As we have already seen, the relatively stable self-sustaining working and business class communities of 1890 had been drastically altered in the fifty years which followed. Industrialization, changing technology, bureaucratization, and consumerism all played a part. The Lynds note that in 1890 there seemed to be a number of plateaus in the stratificational scheme of Middletown life so that a good worker might feel that he was well-off for a person of his sort. By the 1920s, however, "the edges of the plateaus have been shaved off, and everyone lives on a slope from any point of which desirable things belonging to people all the way to the top are in view" (Lynd and Lynd, 1929:83). By 1935 many people realized this was a slope that they could slip down as well as crawl up.

Middletown stratification had changed in one other important way as well. Two families had by their wealth, power, and social style risen well above the rest of the business class. The one which the Lynds call the Y family paid its workers higher than union wages, did not use violent techniques to obstruct union organization efforts, and stayed entirely out of community affairs. In sharp contrast, the X family payed low wages and entered into every aspect of community life. This family was greatly benefited by the Depression because its prime business—the making of glass jars—was very active with the poverty-induced return to home canning. This secure wealth allowed the family to move into diverse areas and enforce its low-wage, anti-union, paternalistic policy.

The interests of the X family nicely illustrate the strategic use of economic power in a community context. The family did not buy into other manufacturing companies in the city; rather it gained power indirectly. The family controlled the *one* bank which survived the bank panic of 1933, it spread its legal business equally among the several leading law firms, and owned the local feeder railroad which connected the main line with the various factories in the city. Thus the family was in a position to exercise monopoly power over credit, legal services, and industrial transportation when any other business interest threatened to disrupt the local labor market or otherwise oppose X family interests. During the Depression, Middletown's leading department store failed because the X family bank would not extend credit. Instead the family took over the store. Two dairies, run by younger members of the family to gain business experience, forced their bigger rival to sell out to them by getting the schools, hospitals, local college and YMCA—all X family charities—to buy only X family milk.

The largest and most profitable X family charity involved the local college.

It had been a small, nearly bankrupt, teachers institute on the edge of town. The family bought the school and all of the surrounding farm land, then donated the school to the state on the provision that it be renamed in their honor and completely rebuilt with state funds. The family had streets paved and sewers laid at city expense, then built fine new homes in the area for family members. They then realized great profit on real estate as other members of the business class hurriedly moved into this newly prestigious area.

Criticism of X family activities and business interests was very unlikely because the family owned the largest daily newspaper and influenced the other by threatening to withdraw advertising. Ministers were more than cooperative, preaching against unionization and the like because all the major denominations were subsidized by the family. "One stubborn 'liberal' minister is reported to have been 'broken' by the family" (Lynd and Lynd, 1937:86). The impressive Masonic Temple was likewise an X family charity. Family members kept a close watch on any outspoken teachers and made forays through the library extracting "radical" books such as John Dos Passos' novel, *1919*.

The X family's control over ideas was neatly illustrated in 1935 when a national labor leader arrived to begin union organization in the factories making automobile parts. The local newspapers would not carry advertisements announcing his meetings. He could not rent any of the large halls in the town, the radio station would not carry his speech even as a paid political announcement, and additional men, whose salaries were presumably paid by the X family foundation, were added to the local police force "in case of union trouble."

The X family was unusually successful in gaining a position of power and prestige. More often the leading families of a community lost power to corporate and governmental interests in the larger cities. The social and economic forces which led to greater centralization of power in the one family in Middletown, however, were very much like those felt everywhere, and it is to an analysis of these forces that we now turn.

ECLIPSE OF COMMUNITY

In a book-length review of community studies spanning the first six decades of the century, Maurice Stein (1960) identifies a general trend which he labels the *eclipse of community*. He sees it as a result of three social processes with which sociologists have long been concerned: urbanization, industrialization, and bureaucratization. Each of these forces is exemplified in the study of Middletown which we have just reviewed.

The eclipse of a geographically delineated community as a meaningful locus for the analysis of industrialization can be further explicated by looking at four institutional areas: technology, economy, polity, and values.

Technology We have already seen how changes in the machinery used in making glass bottles introduced from outside the community made obsolete the skills of trained craftsmen in Middletown. In some cases the livelihood of an entire community is destroyed when a change in technology[2] leads to the closing of a prime industry in a town as happened in the case of many railroad, fishing, and textile mill towns (Aiken et al., 1968). What is more, industrial technology has become so expensive and complex that it cannot be sustained by local money and local human resources. Thus, the community becomes more completely dependent on outside capital, machinery, and trained personnel.

To this point we have talked of technology in terms of tools, machinery, and the technical skills necessary to operate them. But there is another facet to technology as this term has been defined by Marx, Mannheim, and others. It involves both the economy and polity. The other face of technology is the *social organization* which is developed and sustained to successfully operate the machine technology. A specific machine technology does not literally *require* a specific *social technology* but there seems to be a fairly close relationship between the two over time. For example, the machine technology of assembly-line mass production seems to operate most effectively with a social technology of bureaucratic form. This seems to be true whether in an American or Japanese factory, whether in a capitalist, communist, fascist, or Third World nation.

Changes in social technology as well as those in machine technology contributed to the eclipse of community. By the end of the Second World War the social technology of most industrial enterprises had shifted from family-run firms to the corporation. This was true not only of the increasingly large-scale manufacturing industries but also in retail services. Owner-operated groceries, filling stations, drugs stores, etc., were being bought up or were being replaced by corporate chain-stores with centralized management, finance, marketing, and advertising (Preston, 1971). Even the franchise dealerships which first gained prominence in retailing automobiles and spread to service industries by the 1960s leave dealer-owners only a slight scope of managerial autonomy.

The polity Not only was social technology increasingly beyond community influences, but during the same span of time the center of political-legal control of the economic system moved from the community to the federal level. Federal laws governing corporations, workmen's accident insurance, social security, taxation, and labor organizations, as well as numerous federal regulatory agencies (ranging from the Federal Trade Commission to the National Labor Relations Board) shifted the focus of the political economy from the local to the national level. Once this nationalizing focus gained momentum, all interest groups, from industrial firms and trade groups to labor unions and consumer groups, organized on a national level to represent their interests to the federal government in Washington.

Cosmopolitan values A final important realm in which the eclipse of community can be traced is the sphere of communication. The mass media of

2. This use of the term "technology" is drawn from my ongoing research. For a more complete discussion of my use of the concept and a number of other topics mentioned in this work, see Peterson, 1973.

communication—newspapers, radio, telephones, and television—helped to dissolve parochial boundaries between communities, both through the dissemination of news and through the homogenizing effect of advertising. These mass media communications tended to increase the focus of attention on national and international events as well as to homogenize conventions and tastes. We have already discussed the latter in looking at the process of growing "consumerism."

Not only the circulation of information, but also the increasing movement of people from one town to another, has helped the shift from local to cosmopolitan value orientations. The policies of all large corporations and other master organizations, which periodically rotate their personnel from town to town, have also helped greatly to homogenize and cosmopolitanize.

Research alternatives As a result of the processes just discussed, no single geographically bounded community is, by any stretch of the imagination, a representative microcosm of the larger society. Recognizing this changing social reality, researchers interested in the impact of industralization on social institutions and stratification have adopted one or another of four research strategies:

1. They have focused on some particular process, such as the impact of a strike or factory closing on a community (Aiken et al., 1968).
2. They have studied special communities such as middle class suburbs, working class communities, or ethnic neighborhoods (Berger, 1960).
3. They have traced the links between industrialization and a particular institution such as the school, the family, or the church through regional or national surveys without regard to geographical community boundaries (Berg, 1971).
4. They have completely redefined the concept of *community* so that the term refers not to a place where people live and work but to a feeling of collective identity (Nisbet, 1953).

QUEST FOR COMMUNITY

The concern with shared values has a venerable tradition in sociology. Comte and the nineteenth-century sociologists who followed him from Marx to Durkheim feared that the process of industrialization was destroying the sense of communal identity that linked people together. Marx predicted that only socialism could successfully mitigate the destructive consequences of industrialization, while Durkheim looked forward to a state based on a neo-feudal system of industrial guilds.

Community reconceptualized In a book called *The Quest for Community,* Robert Nisbet (1953) notes that both popular writers and sociologists have used the concept "community" as the opposite of estrangement, anomie, alienation, and like terms. In this sense, community refers not to a structurally differentiated functioning social organism but to a sense of shared identity or interests, a consciousness of kind or shared fate. In this sense community is not a *site* for research but a goal to be achieved in the face of the pressure of industrialization to individuate and alienate.

Marx's prediction that class *self*-consciousness is necessary for revolution has energized this conceptualization of community and has led most researchers to define community in class terms. The political implications of his predictions have led several generations of researchers to ask why rapid industrialization has not led to the emergence of revolutionary social class communities. In the process, a great deal has been learned about the dynamics of social class in industrializing societies.

Following roughly the dividing line between business and working class which was employed by the Lynds, researchers focus either on white collar or on blue collar workers. What is more, they tend to focus either on problems of power and exploitation or on problems of style of life and consumption. These distinctions along the lines of class and theoretical concern are convenient bases for organizing the discussion which follows. The numerous essays on the white collar technocrat which have appeared over the last quarter century alloy in differing proportions two distinct diagnoses which were given in nearly pure form several decades ago. The first of these, *The Lonely Crowd,* by David Riesman was published in 1950; the second, *White Collar,* by C. Wright Mills was published a year later. Both focus on social technology and class consciousness but they explain the white collar quest for community in quite different ways. Mills focuses on organizations, polity, and economy, while Riesman focuses primarily on changes in culture and personality.

Owner to employee middle class   Mills traces the emergence of massive industrial corporations, big government, and large-scale organizations generally. The consequences of these changes on social technology are traced in the demise of the old self-employed entrepreneurial middle class and the emergence of the new organization—employee white collar middle class. He sees little alienation in the work of the old middle class of shopkeepers, family farmers, craftsmen, and small manufacturers. Their society is viewed as having a strong family, practical education, self-regulating economy, and an active civil life focused on local community and participatory democracy. Although his view is now widely challenged by social historians, Mills asserts that the world of the small entrepreneurs was self-balancing.

For Mills the central fact of the new middle class is their work in bureaucracies. As bureaucrats each fills a specific position such as "Assistant Office Manager" which is integrated into a vertical chain of command. The bureaucrat holds his position because through education or passing specific tests he has demonstrated competence for his position. He is paid a regular salary and is promoted to positions of greater power, income, and prestige, if he shows that he can follow the rules and conform to the expectations of his superiors in fulfilling his position. Because career is thus defined in terms of a specific corporate organization, and because successful progress involves movement from one company position to another, the white collarite, Mills argues, comes to identify with his employer rather than with the community where he is living at any given time. In this regard, it is interesting to note that careerists in large corporations, the U. S. State Department, universities, the army, and the Catholic church tend to say of their own career-centered world, *"This* is a world apart—unlike the larger world in which it is located."

Mills notes that while the objective work conditions of white collarites are much like those of blue collar workers, they still identify not with the working class but with the interests of top management and corporate capitalism. Since he defines his own job as an area of narrow technical expertise, the white collarite sees politics as the proper domain of specialists other than himself. He becomes "politically indifferent" in sharp contrast to his old middle class counterpart who was continuously engaged in community affairs. Thus, the new white collar classes are seen by Mills as inevitably forming the rear guard of other more articulate political interest groups in society, sometimes following labor, but more often following the lead of corporate interests with which they identify ideologically.

Mills asserts that the new middle class is most likely to follow a strong leader who appeals to its discontent by evoking a politically conservative imagery. Ironically, the same year *White Collar* was published, Senator Joseph McCarthy rose to political eminence by appealing to the sentiments of patriotic anti-communism. McCarthy drew much of his support from white collar classes by successfully channeling their discontent against the scapegoat of an internal communist menace. But such proto-fascism is not the only political reaction that the white collar functionary can make. For example, in the past decade, militant professional associations and trade union organizations have developed rapidly among white collar workers from clerks and government employees to nurses and engineers. What is more, white collarites have been prominent in environmental protection and social reform movements such as that led by Ralph Nader. Whatever the long-term political import of these developments, it is clear that white collarites have become more of a self-conscious community than Mills predicted.

Inner- to Other-Direction   Riesman, like Mills, analyzes changes in American society over the past century. He focuses less on the alienating conditions of work in bureaucratic settings and more on changes in the way the "good life" has been defined and on the concomitant changes in the social institutions of the white collar class community. "Social character" is the key concept for Riesman. It is defined as that aspect of personality which is shared by a wide range of individuals within a given society. He identifies two sorts of social character which are important in America. The first, *inner-direction,* is characteristic of the entrepreneurial middle class, but it has permeated much of the rest of society in the latter half of the nineteenth and the first half of the twentieth century. Inner-direction is an orientation to a set of absolute values and standards of conduct which are implanted in an individual early in life through strict home and school training. These standards impel the inner-directed individual to strive hard and eschew pleasure throughout his life.

Riesman sees another orientation emerging rapidly since World War II in the urban, industrial, organizational environment. He calls this *other-direction*. Other direction is defined as a generalized orientation to seek direction from peers and the mass media. The goals of the other-directed individual shift as these foci of taste-making shift over time. Only the orientation to the tastes of "significant others" endures. Riesman, like Mills, sees white collar work as alienating and sees the flight into consumption as the prime adaptation; unlike Mills, however, he does not view this process as simply a neurotic or pathological escape. Rather, he sees it as basic to a normal and constructive adaptation to the emergence of general affluence. In the home and in progressive schools, other-direction is taught as the ability to understand, fit in, and adjust. It focuses on popularity and style rather than competition and performance. The emphasis on achievement is as great here as ever, but the arena of achievement has changed from production work to consumption, leisure, and politics. In the process, the institutions of family, religion, education, and politics change radically.

While Mills argues that white collarites have not developed a sense of community or class consciousness through work, Riesman argues that they have instead forged a coherent class identity in terms of their extra-work life. He suggests that other-direction provides an orientation which allows persons from diverse backgrounds, who work in widely different industries, and who have moved from one town to another in pursuit of corporate careers to quickly relate to each other and share meaningful social relationships in a community not bounded by space but united by shared orientations to the world of consumption and politics.

Social class and culture class   Recent analysts of the middle class community and institutions do not always follow the lines articulated by Mills on the one hand and Riesman on the other, but they do tend to define their interests either in terms of social class or culture class. Like Mills, the former define white collarites in terms of the way they earn a living. They presume or try to test the ways in which their relationship to the means of production affects other aspects of their lives. While the term *culture class* has not been used before in the literature, it is a convenient term to designate those people who share a common style of *consumption* (Denisoff and Peterson, 1972).

In the early stages of industrialization, when there was widespread scarcity and starvation, social class was clearly most important. For those large segments of the affluent industrial nations who are today well above the level of poverty, culture class probably becomes a more crucial factor. Not only are there a number of radically different ways of spending a $15,000 income, there are cultural choices concerning how much to work and how hard to pursue a career toward conventional goals of success.[3] Whatever

3. This contrast of social and cultural class perspectives may prove useful in illuminating a number of different debates among researchers and politicians. For example, are the

else it may mean, the burgeoning counter-culture of recent years illustrates positive life styles that are clearly at variance with the older culture of success in the job world. While the term culture class is not used, the same split between Riesman's interest in culture class and Mills' interest in social class can be seen in the various studies of the working class community to which we now turn.

Alienation and class consciousness The social class perspective on the blue collarite derives directly from Adam Smith via Marx. In 1776 Adam Smith observed that the repetitive task of factory work gradually robbed the worker of his creative capacity on the job and made him unable to participate fully in the community beyond the factory and work time. Elaborating that economist's observations, Marx, Durkheim, Weber, and others developed the notion that the worker becomes alienated both from the means of production and from community life.

The utility of the alienation theory remains one of the most widely debated subjects among sociologists, but it has been central to researchers taking a social class perspective on the blue collar community (Blauner, 1964; Peterson, 1973:82–89). In a review of the classic works on the subject, Seeman (1959) describes five sorts of alienation. Three of these, powerlessness, meaninglessness, and normlessness, are found widely in blue collar work situations. *Powerlessness* is inherent in those situations where the pace of work and often the quality of work as well is determined by the machines and not the worker. The typical example of such powerlessness is the assembly line. *Meaninglessness* is identified in those situations where the worker cannot see the relationship between the repetitive tasks he performs and the total process of production. Typical of meaninglessness is the job of component-winder for subassemblies which go into esoteric electronic equipment. *Normlessness* occurs in those situations where to perform the job as required a worker must regularly violate generalized norms of good workmanship, safety, health, or honesty. Given the great press for quantity production, these norms are often widely compromised in factory work situations.

Job alienation is theorized to have a number of consequences for work performance. These will be explored in the next part of the text. Here we are concerned with its predicted effect on the working class community. Marx predicted that, in the short-run, job alienation made for a brutish pursuit of escapist leisure. He pointed specifically to alcohol, violence, gambling, and licentious sex. Writing today, he would probably add hard drugs. He also predicted that the working class would increasingly rebel and in the long-run become an increasingly self-conscious class for itself, eventually overthrowing the capitalist class of owners.

---

causes of endemic poverty to be found in the sphere of economic dislocation and exploitation as argued by Blauner (1972) and Wilhelm (1970), or in the culture of poverty practiced by the poor as argued by Moynihan (1965) and Lewis (1966)? Advocates of these two views often argue past each other because they do not recognize that the first defines poverty as a level of income while the other defines it as a style of life.

Numerous scholars have asked why these predictions have not come to pass in the 125 years since Marx made them. Focusing their attention on the situations where job alienation was predicted to be greatest—the most technically advanced segments of industry—researchers in the 1940s and 1950s made numerous studies of auto assembly line workers. A classic study of this sort, entitled *The Automobile Workers and the American Dream,* by Eli Chinoy, was published in 1955. Recent reports in *Life* and *The Wall Street Journal* suggest that very little has changed in the ensuing twenty years. Chinoy found that while workers felt profoundly alienated on the job and realistically saw no great opportunity for promotion out of the blue collar ranks, irrespective of how diligently and intelligently they worked, they did not turn their hostility against their employer or the system at large. In spite of their own experience to the contrary, they continued to believe in "the great American dream" that hardwork and assertiveness can raise any man to the top in our society.

It is interesting to examine the range of mechanisms which help workers maintain this belief in success while they rationalize their own failures. Consumerism, which was discussed above, has been of vital importance. The general standard of living has risen steadily since the Great Depression of the 1930s, so workers can point to advances in their material well-being. Working class families now possess a wide range of material possessions from autos to refrigerators and T.V.'s, none of which was enjoyed by their grandparents. The high value placed on material possessions is evidenced in a number of different ways. For example, a large number of men "moonlight" by holding a second job and, increasingly, their wives seek employment to boost the total family income.

A number of outside agencies devote great effort to maintaining the high levels of consumerism among members of the working class. These include government unemployment benefits, company efforts to stabilize the levels of employment, union efforts to achieve a guaranteed annual income, and government's political choice to reduce unemployment as far as possible even at the cost of a high rate of inflation. While the hardworking blue collarite may not ever join the circle of the rich and powerful, he can, as it says in the ads, live *like* a king.

Having given up the quest for occupational advancement, the average worker devotes a great deal of effort and ingenuity to the achievement of more limited goals which come to be perceived as "really getting ahead." Workers are ingenious at perfecting work habits which satisfy their foremen with a minimum of effort while they scheme to be placed on jobs which are safer, easier, cleaner, quieter, better paying, and relatively immune to unemployment. At the same time, many workers, Chinoy found, define factory work as a temporary means of gaining enough money to establish their own business, whether a filling station, machine shop, or chicken ranch. This goal of self-employment is rarely successfully achieved in practice, for few workers have the talents and knowledge to make a success in the business world. Beyond this, most spend their potential savings on expensive machinery for the house, garden, and their favorite hobbies.

For all this, most older workers will admit they are failures, but they often say that this is not their fault. Some believe their careers were disrupted by war. Many more assert that they labor hard and sacrifice much in keeping a secure but relatively low-paying job rather than taking a big chance on the chicken ranch so that their children can have "all the advantages" they never enjoyed. Research surveys consistently show that workers do not want their children to follow them into the plant; rather they want more education and higher prestige jobs for their offspring. In a sense, then, they project onto their children the responsibility and guilt for their own failure, a theme which has become a major source of intergenerational conflict.

While job alienation may have many consequences, it has not led to the formation of a coherent revolutionary working class community in any highly industrial society. Rather, the factors of community seem to mitigate or compensate for blue collar job alienation. The studies which best explicate this process are written not from the social class but from the culture class perspective to which we now turn.

Embourgeoisment Various recent studies of blue collar families and their suburban communities, made from a culture class perspective, add to the picture of blue collar consumerism which has just been sketched (Berger, 1960; Shostak, 1969; Westley and Westley, 1971; Howe, 1972). Rather than confront the business class, they try to emulate the external features of middle class life styles. Blue collarites choose to spend a great deal of money on their house and yard, using as many labor-saving devices as they can afford. Their hobbies and sports also tend to be capital intensive. These include customized sports cars, expensive guns, boats, and camper trailers. Because of the expense of these items, blue collarites now wish to limit the number of their children to two or three. While they may want college for their children, blue collarites spend less time and money on education than do white collar parents.

For all their new-found affluence gained by persistent work, blue collarites are not content. Their malaise is sometimes expressed through labor union militancy but only to gain higher and more secure incomes. The television programs they watch, as well as the ethos of country music which they increasingly embrace, suggest a yearning to return to a simpler less materialistic era. This desire is given political expression in simplistic nationalism and in the widespread support for populist politicians such as George Wallace.

Religious, national, ethnic, and racial culture distinctions retain a vitality which continues to amaze social scientists who have long believed that these would dissolve in the urban-industrial melting pot. It seems that the embourgeoisment of some elements of the blue collar class requires a belief in the continual proletarian status of other elements of the blue collar community. Thus, while quite similar processes of embourgeoisment can be found among Polish, Black, and Catholic communities, each sees itself as opposing the others in the game of status politics.

The current academic concern with the industrializing community has come a long way from the research tradition which began in the 1920s. Initially researchers such as the Lynds chose a town as a place to study society in microcosm. Using a functionalist perspective which views society as an integrated set of institutions and divided into several classes, they chronicled the complex impact of industrialization on all aspects of community life.

One of the most obvious consequences of industrialization discovered by the early generation of social science researchers was the eclipse of the community by forms of industrialization beyond the control of the community. Students of industrialization were, thus, faced with a choice: either desert the community perspective or entirely reconceptualize the concept of community. A number of researchers in the 1950s and since have redefined community not as a differentiated system located in space but as a set of interests or values of people located at the same position in the class system. Having traced these developments in the community perspective, let us now turn to the orientation which makes the *work place* rather than the community the focus of study.

3 Factory Studies: Productivity and Coordination

As noted at the outset, industrial sociology has addressed six major research questions. The first two have been examined in the section on community. The second two questions are treated in this section.

ORIENTATION

Social technology is focal in the studies made in the work place. In varying degrees they focus on two related questions: (1) How to account for variations in worker productivity? and (2) What forms of organization are most efficient? Framing these questions in terms of productivity is not meant to imply that all researchers work in the interest of management to extract more work from employees. On the contrary, many researchers have been concerned with the exploitation of workers. Nevertheless, it is true that managements have allowed most researchers into factories in hopes of learning how to solve management-defined problems of productivity and efficiency (Baritz, 1960). In a brief review such as this, it is helpful to adopt the management perspective. In the next section, dealing with industry and society, it will be possible to more clearly see the limits of the management perspective on industrial problems.

The systematic study of workers began only in the first decades of this century, but since the early stages of industrialization, factory owners have faced the problem of how to "manage" newly emerging masses of wage workers, most of whom have been peasants or farmers recruited from rural areas quite unused to urban ways of life. The incorporation of wage workers into civil society is of more than historical interest because the two major strategies which were employed, paternalism and fraternalism, are still employed in modified form to this day. The discussion of these strategies also serves as a convenient transition from the chapter on community, because both of these strategies of fostering an able and willing work force focused on building a stable working class community.

Paternalism Paternalism was first systematically put into effect by Robert Owen in his own mills in the early nineteenth century. His writing and lecturing led to the practice being widely copied by other early manufacturers (Bendix, 1956:49–51; Smelser, 1959:106). Owen bought a mill in the countryside and built cottages for his workers; in addition, he built schools, churches, and stores. He provided a police force and town government. He cut the hours of work and guaranteed, as far as possible, regular employment. By providing these extra-work facilities and services, he developed a healthy, sober, loyal, trained, pious, and docile work force. Proud of his achievements, he posed as "father" to his large "family" of workers whom he regarded with "affectionate tutelage."

Seeking to justify this system, paternalism was compared with the lord-serf relationship of feudalism, but in that system the actions of the lord were circumscribed by custom so that he was bound to his serfs nearly as much as they were to him. Free of any such traditional fetters, however, the *industrial* paternalist could be much more arbitrary in his actions. Not only were hours and conditions of work less circumscribed by tradition, but the paternalist could also profit from renting cottages, providing electricity, and operating the community grocery store. What is more, the various institutions of the community could be molded to serve his interests. For example, the school could train manual arts and discipline rather than focusing on academic education, the church could preach a love of authority, docility, and hard work, while the police could enforce the owner's interests and serve as spies, screening new workers and seeking out malcontents. All these exploitative practices and more have been employed by more recent paternalists.

These planned factory towns tend to experience periods of tranquility in relations between the owner-paternalist and the worker-community. These are followed by periods of intense, bitter, and often prolonged labor-management conflict. Nationally prominent strikes of this sort occurred in Pullman, Illinois (1894), the steel towns of western Pennsylvania (1919), Gastonia, North Carolina, a textile mill town (1929–1930), Koehler, Wisconsin, the company town of a plumbing fixture manufacturer (1939–1941 and again in 1954–1960), and in numerous other company towns as well.

Strikes usually begin during a time of economic hardship for the company when it tries to economize by firing workers, reducing wages, and/or increasing workloads. Their income reduced, workers find that they cannot meet rent and grocery store payments, but they reason that the paternalist should continue to supply their life needs. When he does not, the collective discontent generalizes to all aspects of community life in a polarization akin to class warfare. Mass picketing, arson, and bloodshed often occur. The paternalist, believing his own good children to be content, blames "outsiders"—communists, foreigners, Jews, atheists, or other available scapegoats—while he recruits strike-breakers and a private militia. The violence usually stops only when state or federal troops are called to the scene. Such strikes catch paternalists offguard because they expect their "children" to realize that the paternalist is doing all he can for them. Their "childish" uncoordinated rebellion is, however, a predictable reaction to a situation in which one interest controls so many aspects of the life of others and does not let subordinates develop alternate channels of criticism and communication, such as unions, local political parties, newspapers, and the like (Oberschall, 1973).

Seen in historical perspective, the company town was a creative social invention for transforming uprooted peasants and rural immigrants into an industrial laboring class. But, it has been abandoned as generations of more educated, organized, and articulate workers have emerged. Company towns are now found at military bases and in nations just beginning to industrialize. Paternalism of other sorts, however, is still widely practiced in advanced industrial nations as we will see directly.

Fraternalism   If paternalism tries to mold all aspects of working class life, the alternative strategy was to be concerned with none of them. Insofar as they could, these owners defined the only proper relationship with their workers as an exchange of work for wages. Workers are left to develop their own community in interaction with their peers, which is why I have chosen the word *fraternalism* to describe this strategy. The early industrial towns organized in this way were often ghastly ghettos, full of sickness, alcoholism, and all forms of exploitation, but, often with the aid of middle class humanitarians over the course of several generations, the workers evolved an ever more stable working class community life.

Bendix (1956), Smelser (1959), and Mantoux (1961) have traced the development of a fraternal working class community in nineteenth century England. They stress the importance of craft-labor unions, political clubs, fraternal orders, ethnic societies, schools of various sorts, and the working-class-oriented Methodist church in building an independent working class community.

Labor-management tensions are continuous in the fraternalistic situation, but they are arbitrated and accommodated through the various organizations just described so that strikes, when they do occur, tend to be focused on "bread and butter" issues of wages, hours, and working conditions. These strikes are generally short, nonviolent, and do not escalate into major confrontations between the classes, even though the rhetoric of either side may be one of conflict. The well integrated institutional life of Middletown in 1890, which was described earlier, presents a good example of classical fraternalism at the community level.

While no cross-national studies of the incidence of company towns has been made, one would predict that such paternalistic situations are most likely to be found where workers are drawn from systems of plantation agriculture. In Brazil, where this is the case, there is today a large company town of workers, all of whom work for a single banking enterprise. Fraternalism is more likely to emerge where recruits come from independent, small farmers and shopkeepers or where workers can adapt their pre-industrial social structure to factory work situations as has been done with the caste system in India.

PROBLEMS OF PRODUCTIVITY

A number of different strategies have been employed in this century to induce employees to work diligently. Yet most fit within one or another of the four general strategies to be discussed here. The first, *scientific management,* compensates for; the second, *human relations,* accommodates to; while the latter two strategies, *job enlargement* and the *rule of law* in industry, try to overcome objective job alienation. While the first two represent contemporary forms of paternalism, the rule of law represents a contemporary form of fraternalism.

Scientific management At the beginning of this century, the engineers who had been instrumental in creating the technology of mass production turned their attention to the worker. The various movements and activities of the job were divided into minute components and timed in seconds. These activities were then analyzed and reconstituted in more efficient combinations to better utilize the machine technology. Frederick Taylor (1911) was foremost among these human engineers whose techniques came to be called *scientific management.* He was aware of the alienating consequences of trivial work tasks in mass production. In order to encourage the workers full cooperation and interest in doing good work, he proposed compensating the worker for complying with management-established routines by paying him on the basis of the number of units of work he produced. Taylor reasoned that with such incentive pay workers would be motivated to work diligently in order to gain higher wages.

Incentive pay systems have proved to be no panacea in part because they are based on a very naive management view of worker psychology. This is excellently illustrated in a comment made by sociologist Charles Walker: "The chief industrial engineer of the corporation described one day a program which, when completed, would tell every worker in the corporation 'exactly how to do his job down to the last detail. This would serve a psychological as well as a mechanical purpose,' he added. 'Not only will the operators not have to think any more, but they will be much happier on the job and more loyal to the company when we are able to show them that we know so much more about the job than they do' " (Walker, 1962:136). Piecework incentives have been a dominant philosophy of American industrial engineers for the last fifty years, and all industrializing nations, both capitalist and communist, now use a combination of ideological and monetary incentives to motivate workers. Still, the overall proportion of production and related workers participating in individual or group incentive plans has remained relatively constant, at just under 30 percent since the end of World War II.

Workers have generally resisted attempts to measure their productivity. For example, reaction against time-and-motion study engineers was so violent during World War I that a federal law was passed which for thirty years barred all stop-watches from federal munitions plants. While worker resistance has sometimes been a factor, incentive pay plans have not been more widely adopted because in the long run their impact on productivity seems negligible. Ironically, workers who have been taught by scientific management that they were employed to produce rather than to think have turned their creative capacities to beating the incentive system itself. Acting very much like the "economic men" Taylor assumed them to be, workers in most instances have found they can maximize their long-term earnings by producing at a much lower level than they are able. Workers developed the belief that management was always ready to increase the number of work units required for incentive pay while management developed the view that workers were always trying to underproduce. As a result, the incentive system has become a central source of dispute among work groups and a grievance against management rather than the focus of worker-management cooperation that Taylor hoped it would be.

Although the piecework incentive plan was devised by scientific managers to motivate blue collarites, such plans have been most successfully used to motivate while collar salesmen. In most industries, salesmen are paid a low base pay and receive a percentage of all the sales they make as "commission." In addition, special bonuses which are likely to be attractive to the wives of salesmen are given to the most productive workers, thus spurring them to ever greater efforts.

Human relations While scientific management sees work as an engineering problem and asserts an economic basis of motivation, Elton Mayo (1945) and his colleagues at the Harvard Business School in a set of studies begun in the 1930s, have taken a clinical attitude to work and have assumed a psychological basis of worker motivation (Bendix and Fisher, 1949). Their perspective, which is now most widely held in business schools and schools of labor and industrial relations, is called *human relations* in industry. The early studies in this tradition found that when workers were given the *feeling* that they were participating in a managerial decision and were made to *feel* part of a larger work team, they responded with higher productivity and lower absenteeism. These findings seemed like a panacea for management; productivity could be increased with an expenditure of nothing more than charm and human contact. But the long-term effects of this strategy have been a disappointment to management for several reasons.

First, the results of the early studies have been challenged. It has been found that in some instances the higher productivity was simply a function of the increased surveillance over workers during the study, and not a product of management's more humane approach. A number of other studies have shown that worker productivity is only very poorly associated with attitudes toward management, job satisfaction, morale, and other variables, so that the manipulation of these variables can have very little effect on productivity. Second, the more humane ways of treating workers must be *real* to be effective. Where management only *appears* to give workers decision-making power, the hypocrisy itself becomes the focus of added worker disaffection, and their reaction is reminiscent of the worker reactions to classical paternalism.

Third, attempts to increase the commitment to the company have led to the establishment of non-monetary extra-job benefits for workers. These range from company sports teams and picnics, to insurance programs and medical clinics. Rather than increase loyalty to the company, such programs run the risk of being identified as new forms of paternalism which may be approved in the short run as signs of management's concern but are, in the long run, taken to be legitimate parts of the pay package which workers receive. Attempts by management to take away or change these are then subject to the same violent reactions as were found with classical paternalism. In some instances, management has allowed labor unions to administer such programs. While the unions may gain some credit for having "won" benefits, the union is also held responsible for all the individual inequities which particular workers may feel with the system. Thus, while human relations was developed as a way of countering union organization of factories, industrial relations managers today are often able to see to it that management gets credit for a generous system of benefits, while the union gets the blame for individual inequities in its operation (Van de Vall, 1970).

Job enlargement   The third orientation to the problem of productivity has never become a recognized school like scientific management or human relations. Rather, *job enlargement* emerged as a combination of the two earlier schools and its development can be seen in the collection of research papers reprinted by Charles Walker in *Modern Technology and Civilization*. Like scientific management, it focuses on the details of job tasks. But, like human relations, it tries to deal with the job alienation of workers.

As its name implies, the strategy of job enlargement involves the recombination of the various minute tasks of assembly line production into more comprehensive tasks. Thus, a single worker performs a number of different activities in building a complete assembly. This strategy reduces the powerlessness and meaninglessness components of alienation and the early experiments reported remarkably higher productivity and job satisfaction together with less absenteeism and fewer components that were rejected because they failed to pass the inspections of quality control. Based on such results, Walker in 1957 pronounced a "revolution in job design." Yet today job enlargement remains only a minor strategy sometimes employed by industrial engineers. It is not entirely clear whether this promising technique in the manipulation of social technology has not spread because of the constraints of machine technology or because of the resistance of workers, unions, managers, or engineers.

Like most experiments designed to demonstrate some commercially valuable time or money-saving invention, however, researchers usually terminate their experiment and publish their results soon after they have positive findings. They do not wait to see how the strategy works in the long run or works under ordinary shop conditions. In the case of job enlargement, workers may reject it in the long run because of one of its supposed benefits—higher quality production. Since total components are produced by a single worker it is easy to fix the blame for poor workmanship. In such blue collar situations, workers may well prefer the anonymity of an alienating assembly line to the competition and responsibility of job enlargement, where workers are likely to be sanctioned by their fellows if they produce too much or too well and fired by management if they produce too little.

Rule of law While the three strategies just described were created by managers, engineers, and social scientists focusing on the machine and the worker, another approach has emerged since the 1930s out of the conflictual struggles of management, workers, and labor unions. State and federal governments have played a crucial role in its development. This approach is quite distinct from human relations and scientific management in its assumptions about why men work and how to achieve productivity, but it is not usually defined in academic circles as a separate or distinct school of labor-management relations. Elsewhere (Peterson, 1973:92–95) I have called this approach the *rule of law* in industry, because it employs the mechanisms of the legal system on the assumption that when workers are able to bargain with management, they will willingly give a fair day's work for a fair day's wage.

The New York State law was the model but the National Labor Relations Act of 1934 now forms the cornerstone of rules on industry. Through it, industrial workers have gained the right to bargain collectively with management over wages, hours, and working conditions. Thus, what had often been a bloody struggle to organize workers into unions became more nearly a contest between management and unions to attract the loyalty of workers, with the National Labor Relations Board (NLRB) acting as referee to see that neither side intimidated workers. Besides setting the rules and acting as referee, government may be called upon to mediate and arbitrate differences between the various parties.

In recent years, union representation elections have largely replaced the bombings, goon squads, industrial sabotage, labor spies, and strike-breakers of an earlier era. Over the years there has developed a system of rules and procedures forming a framework within which power contests between the various parties can be decided without resorting to violence. At issue has been the unions' right to negotiate wages, seniority rights, work quotas, pension rights, and related working conditions. But in recent years wider issues of equity have emerged. For example, these include questions about the extent to which workers with seniority in one plant of a firm have a right to good jobs in a new plant being built by that firm at a distant location. The continuous discussion between the parties involved has tended to shift the focus to wider questions of equity, and each party has come to recognize that its own interest is best served when the other parties are prospering and satisfied.

The further development of such labor-management cooperation on the basis of mutually understood equities is largely precluded by the societal context within which negotiations typically take place. On the other hand, corporation managers are expected by their profit-minded shareholders to keep wages as low as possible, while on the other hand, workers expect their elected union representatives to get every possible penny in wages. Thus, an atmosphere of hostile antagonism is fostered and perpetuated by union and management rhetoric to satisfy the expectations of each side. The continued staging of this political drama prevents the rule of law from becoming the basis of more creative labor-management relations.

Although there has been an unending stream of studies dealing with relationships among technology, pay, job satisfaction, motivation, and pro-ductivity over the past fifty years, the results seem to be contradictory and inconclusive. Seen in retrospect, most of the research data have been in-terpreted to confirm a predrawn conclusion rather than evaluated in the spirit of open-minded scientific inquiry. Partly for this reason, industrial relations, which in the 1950s was the focus of attention of a great many sociologists, has now largely faded from academic research interests to be carried on in business and industrial labor relations schools which are more interested in the control of workers. At the same time, firms around the world have begun to experiment with a number of different plans which give workers more freedom to fit work into the rest of their activities. No systematic research has been made of these diverse experimental efforts. But increasingly during the 1950s and 1960s, factory sociology turned from a study of the worker to a study of work organization.

PROBLEMS OF ORGANIZATIONAL COORDINATION

In the early stages of industrialization, an owner could know all of his workers and oversee their work more or less directly. As the number of employees has grown from a few dozen to a few thousand, the problems of coordination have grown correspondingly. We have already noted the shift from family businesses and craft production methods to corporate forms utilizing bureaucracy. This change has been the major strategy for solving the problems of coordination of larger numbers of workers. Unfortunately, bureaucracy has developed many of the pathologies that Weber feared, rather than become the organizational panacea he had hoped it would become.

Empirical study of the forms and pathologies of organization began early in this century, and the analysis of organizations has absorbed the interest of more sociologists than any other single topic during the past thirty years. The findings of these researchers are tremendously diverse, and in this brief summary we can only touch on those aspects of organizational studies which most explicitly deal with the problems of coordination in industrial organization.

Rational organization, irrational individual After Weber, perhaps the most influential writer on industrial organization was Chester Barnard, one-time president of the New Jersey Bell Telephone Company. In *The Functions of the Executive,* published in 1938, he argued that the industrial organization is a system of *cooperation* oriented to the common good of all participants—management, labor, and consumers alike. His formulation of organizational relations relies on a theory of human psychology very much like that of the early human relations theorist, Elton Mayo. Believing that organizations are cooperative systems which workers join voluntarily to achieve common rational goals, all those actions of individual workers or groups which are at variance with management directives are considered by Barnard to be unconscious or irrational acts of rebellion (Perrow, 1972). This formulation represents another example of modern-day paternalism, for management is presumed to be omnipotent and omniscient in organizational affairs, and workers are expected to express their fealty.

The many researchers who have been schooled in this tradition are trained to define defects in coordination as deriving from the threatened egos and unfulfilled psychological needs of individuals and groups in the organization, rather than deriving from legitimate differences of opinion, exploitation, and the like. Most contemporary management consultants use this perspective, although there have been two major changes in the emphasis of these "organizational doctors" over time. First, where they began by focusing their attention on the coordination problems caused by blue collar workers, they now focus more often on those problems caused by middle- and upper-management. Second, where they began by trying to adjust the individual to the needs of the organization, some of them are now more likely to try to adjust the structure of the organization to more nearly fulfill the presumed psychic needs of individuals (Bennis and Slater, 1968).

Decision theory While the followers of Barnard have been concerned with organizational versus individual needs, another school of researchers has examined organizational rationality from the perspective of the mathematical theory of games. Herbert Simon's 1956 book, *Models of Man,* converted the sterile propositions of gain theory into a set of testable propositions. Both individuals and organizations are seen as *intending* to act rationally in serving their own interests. Insofar as they are not rational in achieving their own ends, it is because their choices are quite circumscribed. They must act on incomplete information, without being able to take time for a complete investigation of alternatives, with less than the necessary resources, in a situation where there are already prior commitments to particular solutions, and only a limited range of alternatives are defined culturally as possible, wise, legal and/or ethical. Under such conditions, which Simon presumes to be the usual case in business, decision makers cannot make the "optimum" decisions but search for one which "satisfices," that is, the first solution found which is believed to be adequate for the problem at hand.

Decision theorists have been able to research and codify a number of propositions about organizational processes, but this promising perspective has received surprisingly little attention from sociologists. This may well be because while it was being codified during the mid-1950s, organizational sociologists were almost totally preoccupied with studying the internal dynamics of organizational bureaucracy, and they were unwilling to take into account the various factors in the organization environment to which the decision theory calls attention. As we will note shortly, this perspective of organizational sociologists is now very much changed.

Pathologies of bureaucracy During the 1940s and 1950s most organizational sociologists were in one way or another concerned with testing Weber's assertion that bureaucracy is the most efficient form of coordination. The classic academic study in this tradition was made by the political analyst, Robert Michels, who in 1915 showed that even the political parties most committed to participatory democracy come to be run by their inner core of full-time party functionaries. He found that, over time, the party comes to reflect the interests of this bureaucratic cadre and not the total membership. Michels' "iron law of bureaucratization" has been the touchstone of many lines of research, six of which will be mentioned here. First, Merton (1968:249–260), following the lead of novelists from Dostoevsky to Kafka, has found that bureaucratic functionaries, rewarded for following the rules to the letter, become unable to adapt to changed situations. They develop what he ironically terms a "trained incapacity" to adapt. Second, Blau (1955) has refined this point to show that workers do not try to achieve the goal set for their job. Rather, they work to fulfill only those expectations which are most easily quantifiable and thus those which are used by supervisors in making evaluations. Blau has shown that when the means of evaluating performance is changed there is a corresponding change in how employees perform their jobs.

Third, bureaucratic rules are generated to circumscribe the discretion and power of officials, but these officials may use the rules to help or frustrate other persons or groups who depend on them. Thus, as Gouldner (1952) has shown, "red tape" may be spun or cut at the discretion of bureaucratic functionaries to serve their own ends. Mechanic (1962) has described how the control which strategically located lower-level organizational participants have over the day-to-day flow of information in the organization, gives them much more power than is apparent from simply looking at the formal organizational rules governing their jobs.

Fourth, in a large-scale study of the Tennessee Valley Authority, Selznick (1949) shows that in many instances what may appear as "red tape" or bureaucratic ineptitude is in fact part of the systematic efforts of organized groups to control aspects of the organization. He also found that in many cases these groups are located outside the organization entirely. This "interpenetration" of organizations is often a deliberate strategy in which one organization gives outsiders some power in the organization on condition that they facilitate the organization in achieving its goals. This process he called "cooptation." In practice it is often not clear which group has more successfully coopted the other. Fifth, Gouldner (1954a, 1954b) has shown that when the level of formal bureaucracy is increased in a factory to improve coordination, new problems of coordination arise and additional bureaucratic rules are introduced. Thus, there is initiated a vicious circle of increasing bureaucratization. His studies dramatically show some of the factors which account for the iron law of bureaucratization first outlined by Michels. Unlike Michels, however, Gouldner asserts that increasing bureaucratic rules is but one strategy and is not inevitable.

Finally, in a study of the printing industry, Lipset, Trow, and Coleman (1956) show that the Printers Union had retained a high degree of participatory democracy over a great number of years. Their findings seem to fly in the face of the "iron law" and give credence to Gouldner's view that the form of organization is not fated but a matter of human choice. When they made their Printers Union study, however, the industry was quite unusual in its machine technology. Even in the 1950s it operated with a technology using master craftsmen performing skilled handwork, a machine technology which had been replaced in most industries thirty years earlier. Since their study was made, the printing industry has undergone massive changes in machine technology. While no systematic restudy has been made, the craft union has apparently lost much of its power and much of its democracy as well. In this light, the printing industry seems less of an exception to the iron law of bureaucratization and more an illustration of the close links between machine and social technology. Their interdependence was sometimes noted in earlier studies, but not until the 1960s did machine technology enter as a major explanatory variable in the relationship between organizational form and effective coordination.

Technology and coordination As Faunce (1968) has noted, the development of machine technology can be divided into several phases which have developed in historical succession. These include: first, handicraft production such as in printing shops or the first Middletown glassware factories discussed earlier; second, the application of inanimate sources of power to the production process and the consequent building of ever larger single-purpose machines such as those found in the textile industry; third, the development of machinery for materials handling and the redesign of machinery into assembly lines such as those in the automobile industry; and, finally, the mechanization of quality control and decision making as exemplified by the computers and other related paraphernalia of automation which are beginning to be introduced in a wide range of industries from insurance to petroleum.

Blauner (1964) uses a parallel analytical division of machine technology in a reanalysis of a wide range of industrial studies. He identifies the same four stages of machine technology and links each with a specific social technology and level of subjective alienation. Reviewing these studies and incorporating more recent findings, Peterson (1973) relates the changes in machine and social technology to changes in the organization of firms and the processes of industrialization in the larger society beyond the factory. While some of the philosophical critics of technology, including Ellul (1964), fear a technological *determinism,* the empirical research has increasingly shown that technological innovations require a wide range of organizational, social, cultural, and economic *pre*conditions.

Coordination and environment   As we have seen, the systematic study of organizational coordination began by asking how organizations can best control the activities of their members—an internal problem. But, this line of inquiry has increasingly come to focus on the importance of organized groups *beyond* the firm in determining organizational coordination.

Labor unions are perhaps the most obvious example of an organized environmental influence on industrial coordination and yet, to a degree which now seems remarkable, early academic researchers tended to ignore their influence and even excluded them entirely from consideration. Beginning about 1950, studies of labor influences focused on union-management conflict. By that time the great new industrial labor unions organized through the CIO had consolidated the power they had won in the New Deal of the late 1930s and in the Second World War. In part reflecting the changing realities of union-corporation relations, more recent studies such as that of Van de Vall (1970) have shown that the increasing rule of law in industry has led to the cooptation of labor unions by the corporation. The rhetoric of competition to the contrary notwithstanding, labor unions have tended to become, in effect, part of the industrial relations department of the corporation.

The complexity of the relations between management and unions is dramatically illustrated in a study by Chandler (1964). She found in the firm she studied that one major element of management was in conflict with another and that each was closely allied with one of two major labor unions which were competing for the jobs in the work situation. These lines of cleavage within management which allied elements of management with elements of labor were not based on short-run clashes of personality or power seeking. Rather, they were based on the long-term interests of the various factions based on occupational competence, technological commitments, and other similar structural variables.

That Chandler's findings are not based on factors special to the situations she studied is suggested by a host of recent studies which show how organizational structure is affected by various elements in the environment. Taken together, they show that, contrary to Weber's assertion, bureaucracy is not always the most efficient form of organization. The environmental conditions favoring craft administration (Stinchcombe, 1959), professional administration (Perrow, 1967), and entrepreneurship (Peterson and Berger, 1971) have been explored. Thompson (1967) and Zald (1970) have developed general schemes in an effort to predict the impact of various elements such as rival firms, competing products, government rules and laws, finances, etc., on the form and effectiveness of organizational coordination. If these suggest nothing else, they imply that the most important determinants of productivity and coordination lie beyond the work place.

There is a striking parallel between the development of the industry-in-community and the factory orientation with which we have been concerned. Both began with studies defined narrowly within the tradition. But, later studies have pointed to the importance of factors beyond the confines of each orientation. Earlier we noted the eclipse of the community orientation. It now seems quite appropriate to suggest that there has been a parallel *eclipse* of the factory orientation in industrial sociology. As in the case of the community orientation, the eclipse has been caused by changes in the larger industrial society beyond the purview of the particular orientation. Facing this larger societal reality for the first time in fifty years, the empirical industrial sociologists have begun in the past several decades to take industrializing society *itself* as the focus of study. In a very real way, then, sociology has come full circle, for as we have noted, sociology began as the analysis of the consequences of the continuing industrial revolution on society at large.

4   Industrializing Society

Increasingly since the mid-1950s sociologists have become concerned with the industrialization of whole societies. What is more, those engaged in research on more limited topics now often take into account the nation as economic, political, and social context. This emerging *industrializing society* approach, as we shall call it, addresses the final pair of the six major research questions of industrial sociology which were enumerated at the outset: (1) the factors which shape the development of industrialization, and (2) the impact of industrialization on various societal problems. In practice, the causes and consequences of industrialization are not usually so neatly differentiated. Rather, researchers have tended either to concentrate on the cross-national comparison of modernization or have linked industrialization to some particular societal problem such as pollution, racial conflict, or the future of work.

COMPARATIVE PERSPECTIVES

Contemporary sociological concern with the comparative analysis of industrialization grew directly out of the study of labor-management relations. Nowhere is this so graphically illustrated as in Reinhard Bendix's (1956) four-nation study, Work and Authority in Industry.[4]

Bendix: managerial ideology and societal commitments In many ways Bendix's study ranks with the work of Lynd and Lynd as a classic. To summarize his perspective would be to review much of what we have already discussed. For example, he examines the links between industrialization and the various institutions of society; industrialization's impact on stratification; various managerial strategies (paternalism, scientific management, human relations); and also the link between changing machine technology and bureaucratization. By looking at data of four different industrializing nations in time perspective, he is able to incorporate both the community and the factory approaches for studying industrializing society. For our present purposes, at least, Bendix's major contribution is to argue that societies show great continuity over time in values and institutional arrangements in spite of the revolutionary changes wrought by industrialization. While he examines data from four countries he, in effect, looks at two alternate paths of industrialization. The "Western" path includes early industrialization in England and contemporary industrialization in the United States, while the "Eastern" includes Czarist Russia and contemporary East Germany.

Bendix contrasts the two paths in a number of ways. In the West, industrialization was inaugurated by a broad class of entrepreneurs; in the East, by the plan of Czar Peter and his followers. In the West, wage-laborers were employed. In the East, serfs, who were obligated by custom and law to do their masters' bidding, became the factory workers. In the West, there was an ideology of "free enterprise," where individually negotiated contracts increasingly replaced customary relations. In the East, the ideology of Czarist involvement in the affairs of master and serf was reaffirmed. Thus, while in the West the government often acted in the class interest of the industrialist, in the East the government regularly

4. More than any other single work, Bendix's book helped direct my attention to the long-term process of industrialization in societal context. Likewise, Alvin Gouldner's work captivated me in graduate school and the Middletown books, as interpreted by Maurice Stein, drew me into sociology as an undergraduate. Together, these influences form the foundation on which this book has developed.

intervened in disputes between industrialists and workers. By the twentieth century the prime ideological incentive for work in the West had become "equal opportunity to achieve individual rewards through hard work and competition," while in the East the prime ideological incentives had become "each works for the good of all as embodied in the Socialist State."

A number of critics have found the East-West polarization to be over-drawn. Some have argued this derives from Bendix's explicit commitment, which was fashionable among academics in the mid-1950s, to laud capi-talism and condemn communism. This charge of unscholarly partisanship is not unfounded, for the book concludes with the assertion that: "The task of this study has been to examine the institutional and ideological elements which comprise the cumulative commitments and arsenal of ideas on both sides of the Iron Curtain. There are more assets in the West and more liabilities in the Russian tradition than have yet been brought to the fore" (Bendix, 1956:449).

This statement was removed from the 1963 paperback edition, but many would still not be satisfied with the East-West polarization. Some re-searchers would dispute the importance of ideology or social structural commitments. They would substitute economic, or demographic, or tech-nological, or cultural, or psychological factors in explaining both the rise of industrialization and the route of continuing modernization. This ca-cophony of alternative explanations is frustrating to one seeking a single answer, but exhilarating to one interested in contributing to the fund of human knowledge. This excitement can be traced to several factors. First of all, where there is confusion on a major issue, there is a possibility of a major theoretical advance. Second, where there is such a surfeit of ideological confrontation between scholars as exists on this issue, it is likely that the questions at hand are vital in the workings of society. The analysis of the various theories of industrialization and modernization can fill whole books (Moore, 1963; Frank, 1972). In the brief space available here, we will sketch three alternatives to the Bendix approach.

Consequences of social technology Many sociologists would use the same set of variables as Bendix, but place different stress on their causal influence. Ideology, values, and the like, for example, are often treated as dependent consequences of changes in technology and social struc-ture. Barrington Moore's study of the *Social Origins of Dictatorship and Democracy* (1966) is an excellent case in point. Moore bases his theory on data from the early stages of industrialization in seven major industrial nations. In each case, he finds industrialization began in agriculture, and the labor-management relations which are established there have far-reaching consequences.

In those nations where few workers were required by the technology of agricultural production, as for example in England and France, peasants were forced off the land. Their expropriation was rationalized and legal-ized in ways which became the basis for the later claims of freedom, equality, and democracy. In those nations where many workers were required by the technology of agricultural production as in Germany and Japan, the feudal customs which tied the peasants to the land were reinstated or strengthened. This set in motion industrialization by the feudal aristocracy, and the process came to be rationalized by ideologies of a fascist sort. Viewed in the light of this analysis, the American Civil War can be seen as a contest between democracy and proto-fascism. It pitted Northern advocates of technology-intensive industrialization and independent Midwestern farmers against Southern advocates of a labor-intensive plantation system. In those nations like Russia and China where industrialization has successfully taken place only in the wake of world war and a socialist revolution, industry along with the rest of society has been organized along communist lines.

Moore's argument is not as deterministic as this brief synopsis makes it appear. Nevertheless, more than most sociologists, he stresses the importance of the social technology of agricultural production, which in turn depends on the geography and climate of a region, which favors the commercial exploitation of one sort of crop or another, for later political and ideological developments. Sociologists, including the evolutionists to be considered next, more often have considered changes in social relations and ideology as *pre*requisite to successive stages of the industrial revolution.

Evolution by differentiation   As noted in section one, the idea of societal evolution has been central from the earliest days of sociology. The recently revived interest in the cross-national comparison of industrialization has brought evolutionary perspectives back to the fore. Structural differentiation is one of the prime mechanisms which evolutionists use to describe and explain industrialization. For example, Talcott Parsons (1964, 1966) has described the development of four institutional systems which were essential prerequisites to the industrial revolution. Each emerged by differentiation from prior simpler forms. These include the bureaucratic form of organization which replaced kinship as the prime basis of social technology, the evolution of money markets out of a barter system, the codification of a universalistic legal system, and the differentiation of democratic political organizations which evolved in the contest between the landed nobility and the rising urban commercial class of merchants.

The differentiation view has been challenged on a number of grounds (cf. Eisenstadt, 1964, 1966; Frank, 1972) but perhaps the most telling is that it often remains a description of change without a clear explanation of the processes involved. While his study is not comparative like the others reviewed in this section, the most nearly explanatory analysis of the process of differentiation is that made by Parsons' student, Neil Smelser, in his (1959) study of *Social Change in the Industrial Revolution.*

Smelser's view is one of "tension management." He finds that differentiation takes place in a seven-stage sequence which applies equally well to the process of technological innovation in industry *and* to the adaptation of the family to changes brought by industrialization. For Smelser the process begins when an outside element disrupts the ongoing system; tensions are expressed; they are more or less roughly suppressed; but experimental attempts to innovate go on behind the scenes; one or more of these experiments is defined as successful, it quickly replaces the older process; and, in time, it becomes the routine, the accepted norm. In this way structurally simpler and more homogeneous social structures evolve into more complex and differentiated systems. We have already met with several situations that might conveniently be interpreted in these terms. Recall, for example, the differentiation of various institutions out of the early all-encompassing family of Middletown.

Scarcity and surplus Economists, demographers, and statisticians tend to look at the process of industrialization in quite quantitative input-output terms. Their variables include the dynamics of population, the range of natural resources, techniques of capital formation, labor productivity, patterns of consumption, and the like. They tend to take sociocultural factors as given and some, including Ogburn (1933), presume that bio-economic factors are not only necessary but also sufficient for industrialization.

One of the most "sociological" of these theorists, because he deals with the social and ideological requisites of industrialization, is the economist W. W. Rostow. In his review of the *Stages of Economic Growth* (1960), Rostow identifies five stages of industrialization. The *first,* the preindustrial or "traditional" society, may be far from static, but the system is caught in a cycle of expansion, war, subjugation, plunder, and decay. A very high proportion of all resources is necessarily devoted to agricultural production. Because there is no systematic application of resources to new technologies, there is a practical ceiling on the obtainable output per man hour. While there may be a central government, power is held by the landed aristocracy, and there is a pervasive value system which Rostow describes as long-run fatalism.

In the *second,* "transitional" stage, economic progress is for the first time defined as both possible and desirable. In most cases, this change is induced by the example and threat of more advanced nations. By appeal to religion, patriotism, profit, and force, individuals and groups are induced to reinvest much of the small surplus available in more productive technologies, systematic exploitation of available natural resources, aids to commerce, technical education, and the like. Rostow notes that the decisive feature in this stage is the development of a national government which can effectively nullify the domination of the landed aristocracy through changes in law and governmental administration. Often this is accomplished by appeals to new sentiments of nationalism.

The *third* stage, which Rostow calls "take-off," is crucial for the continued development of industrialization. At this point the forces making for economic progress come to dominate the society, and without great sacrifice it is possible to reinvest ten percent of all income in capital development. Thus, economic growth becomes the *normal* condition and the development toward later phases of industrialization is insured. The *stalled* development of a number of industrializing nations, most notably Argentina, however, has caused a number of researchers to question Rostow's assertion that post take-off development is inevitable (Peterson, 1973:17–18). The *fourth* stage is called "drive to maturity." While take-off is usually initiated by the rapid expansion of one major industry, economic maturity comes as other sectors of the economy catch up with the leading sector.

The *fifth* stage, that of "high mass consumption," is reached when enough goods are produced so that all in the society are able to live well above the level of survival. In this stage, the society is faced with a new range of choices concerning how to allocate the resources which the fantastically productive technology produces. Rostow enumerates three alternatives: (1) the development of ever higher levels of consumption goods and services; (2) the elaboration of health and welfare services; and (3) investment in increasingly expensive warfare technology and the pursuit of international power and influence. While all advanced industrial societies "buy" some of each, Rostow asserts that the United States has opted primarily for high levels of consumption, Western Europe has opted primarily for welfare, and Russia has opted primarily for war technology and foreign adventure. In the light of his analysis, it is interesting to note that soon after his study, which had the subtitle, "A Non-Communist Manifesto," was completed, Rostow became the Special Advisor for Foreign Affairs to Presidents Kennedy and Johnson. In this capacity, he became a prime architect of America's massive investment in the Vietnam war. The inflationary impact of this war has curtailed the rise in consumption and welfare expenditures in the United States.

While many analysts now see the Vietnam war as a $200,000,000 mistake, some economists like Baran and Sweezy (1966) see much military adventures as *inevitable* in the later stages of advanced capitalism. Like Rostow, they begin with the assumption that the problem of advanced industrialization such as the United States is how to *distribute* the great amounts of surplus which derive from the highly efficient technology. Baran and Sweezy presume that any significant redistribution of the surplus to the poorer segments of the society is impossible because it would threaten the hegemony of the political and economic powers that be. They show that surplus is (1) reinvested in further scientific and technical advancement, thus creating further surplus; (2) expended on competition among corporations through model changes and advertising; (3) sunk in planned obsolescence so that products are designed in such a way that they will soon need to be replaced; and (4) increasingly invested in military technology and foreign adventure. A decade ago, the Baran and Sweezy interpretation of the dilemma of the era of high mass consumption was dismissed by almost all industrial sociologists as "communist ideology." But today the industrializing society approach is undergoing a rapid transformation which brings to the fore questions like those raised by Baran and Sweezy. It is this new concern to which we now turn.

EMERGING PERSPECTIVES

In recent years, analysts of industrialization have increasingly turned from the study of whole nations to a more microscopic analysis of some particular phase, process, or social problem. Many of these are studies which hark back to the community and factory perspectives discussed earlier. Most differ from their earlier counterparts in three important ways, however. First, they take advantage of a rich reservoir of historical and statistical data not previously available. Second, many utilize new and powerful computer-dependent techniques of analysis. Finally, most ask research questions which are less parochial and more continually informed by the community, factory and society perspectives simultaneously.

Current research being conducted by Britt and Galle neatly illustrate these tendencies. Using sophisticated computer-dependent techniques to analyze statistical data spanning more than twenty years, they are trying to isolate the causes of industrial conflict in the United States by examining strike data on twenty major industries in each of one hundred cities. Their findings to date (cf. Britt and Galle, 1972) suggest that the technology of the industry, degree of unionization, type of community, as well as general economic factors, help to explain variations in a propensity to strike.

But the emerging perspective in industrial sociology is not just an amalgamation of its predecessors. Rather, the organizing idea is that specific phenomena in the industrial realm can best be understood in terms of more encompassing demographic, technological, economic, governmental, social, and cultural factors. These are redolent of the set of factors deemed important by Adam Smith, the eighteenth-century economist whose work we discussed at the outset. A bewildering range of studies and experiments are currently being made by men of affairs as often as by scholarly researchers. Three general areas of current interest will be discussed here: the future of work, occupational discrimination, and the control of corporate enterprise. They have been chosen because they illustrate studies deriving primarily from the factory, community, and societal perspectives respectively.

The future of work   From time to time, the prediction is made that new machine technology is obviating the need for human labor. As long ago as 1853, for example, a writer in the *United States Review* predicted that the day will come when "machinery will perform all work, automata will direct them. The only task of the human race will be to make love, study, and be happy." When that prediction was made, 33 percent of the total United States population was gainfully employed. But 117 years later, in 1970, the comparable figure was 36 percent—hardly a shift to universal leisure! Thanks to innumerable technological changes over the past century, however, human labor has been made much more productive. While some of this increased productivity has gone to shorten the work week, most of it has been invested in raising the standard of living.

If he returned today, our author of 1853 might argue that the millennium had almost arrived, for most people today are engaged in occupations he would not recognize as work. In 1850, 66 percent of all workers were engaged in agriculture, forestry, or mining, and half of the remainder were employed in manufacturing. Today a bare 4 percent of all workers are engaged in agriculture, forestry, and mining, and just 25 percent are employed in manufacturing. In 1850 there were a few teachers, professionals, domestic servants, tradesmen, and government workers, but now this heterogeneous service sector of the economy includes a host of new occupations and engages 64 percent of all those gainfully employed in the civilian labor force. Another major shift in employment is the place of women in the labor market. In 1850 fewer than one in ten workers were women, while today women comprise one-third of the gainfully employed.

Most industrial sociologists have been slow to recognize these and other changes in the world of work. An exception is Sheppard and Herrick's (1972) study which has the suggestive title, *Where Have All the Robots Gone?* They find the male worker is discontented with the alienating conditions of work, estranged from the labor union which is supposed to represent him, and troubled about the community and society which seems to fate his children to a future much like his own.

This discontent is expressed by men like Gary Byner, the 30-year-old president of the United Automobile Workers Local at General Motor's strike-plagued Vega plant in Lordstown, Ohio, which was recently built as a model of automated efficiency. With the help of computers, engineers designed the assembly line to produce one hundred automobiles an hour. This rate is almost twice as fast as the conventional line, giving each worker under forty seconds to complete his task. Under this pressure, both machines and men have failed. Charles Camp (1972) of the *Wall Street Journal* notes, "In the past two months, incomplete and damaged cars have been coming off the assembly line so fast that repair yards are often choked before an eight-hour work shift is much more than half over." As Byner says, "A guy goes home dead-assed tired from a dead-assed job. So what happens? It used to be that when he got home he was the father, the head of the family, the man, now he just hands over the check. He's got to strike out. He's going to strike out at the company. He's going to strike out at the union. He's going to strike out at women. He's going to strike out in politics" (Harris, 1973).

This discontent has not converted workers into rebels. Instead, it has led them, together with management, to seek novel ways of increasing productivity while humanizing work at the same time. Of course, worker-management cooperation often comes only under dire economic threat. For example, when Kaiser Steel Corporation announced that it would close part of its Fontana, California plant because it could not produce steel at a competitive price, the workers together with local management asked for the chance to make changes in the machinery and work assignments. The large number of minor changes resulted in a productivity increase of 32 percent! (*Time,* 1973).

In recent years, a number of small- and middle-sized firms have found ingenious ways of increasing productivity by taking into account the interests and skills of their workers. Most of the devices, such as profit-sharing, job enlargement, joint worker-management committees, and the like, are not new. The new component is the greater willingness to experiment with less ideological concern over "management prerogatives" or "class interests." Illustrative of this tendency is the manipulation of the work week. While some firms experiment with a three-day week, others have moved to alternating 70-hour seven-day work weeks with a full week off. An increasing number of firms in this country and in Germany now let workers set their own hours within broad limits. In most cases, these changes have been made in firms employing great numbers of women who traditionally had high rates of absenteeism and tardiness because of the joint demands of home and work. With the ever rising levels of affluence, people are not so compelled to seek any available employment just to avoid starvation. Increasingly managers must redesign work situations to make them attractive. The variable work day just described is only one of a number of examples that might be cited. Higher up the occupation scale, work incentives seem to be changing as well in ways that are not yet well understood but seem to reflect the shift, discussed earlier, from inner-direction to other-direction.

Occupational discrimination   If the nature of work is shifting, the differential access of some people to good jobs on the basis of their race, sex, ethnicity, social class, and age is not changing so rapidly. In recent years, there has been increased research on the extent and causes of job discrimination against women. But discrimination against Blacks has received the greatest sustained attention. And three studies in this area will be used to illustrate the range of approaches to the sudy of occupational discrimination.

In 1970, Sidney Wilhelm published a work with a provocative title, *Who Needs the Negro?* He views Blacks as the most recent major ethnic group to immigrate to the urban industrial North of the United States. Earlier generations of Irish, Swedish, Italian, and Polish peasant immigrants found laboring and unskilled blue collar jobs in industry and moved up the skill hierarchy over the years so that their children and grandchildren have become socially indistinguishable from the earlier Anglo-Saxon immigrants. A similar path toward job integration might have been followed by Blacks, Wilhelm argues, but they immigrated to the industrial North at a time when most menial jobs were being eliminated by increasingly sophisticated technology. What is more, the nontechnical jobs which remained had become dead ends rather than training grounds for better jobs. Thus, Blacks have been unable to follow the well-worn path of social integration through improved jobs. Much of Wilhelm's book is devoted to detailing the mechanisms used to cope with the "oversupply" of unemployable Blacks.

In a recent work, Blau and Duncan (1967) argue that job discrimination against Blacks may primarily result from factors beyond the changing "job mix" in American society. Using a Census Bureau sample of over 20,000 men, they analyze among other things the sources of job discrimination against Blacks. Blacks tend to come from impoverished homes in the South and have an inferior education. "Yet even when these differences are statistically analyzed and we examined how Negroes would fare if they did not differ from whites in these respects, their occupational chances are still inferior to whites" (Blau and Duncan, 1967:238). Thus, there is a clear residual of discrimination. Of particular note is their finding that the greater their education, the greater the difference between Blacks and whites in occupational achievement. Thus, better educated Blacks suffer the greatest discrimination, or put the other way, education is a much better investment for whites than for blacks.

The Blau and Duncan study has opened up a whole range of further research into the causes of discrimination. Edna Bonacich (1972), for example, has looked at what she calls a "split labor market" such as those found in a number of areas around the world. According to her processual formulation, an economically disadvantaged ethnic or racial group offers its services at a pay level well below that of the dominant group. Its willingness to work for low pay may, but need not, derive from prior discrimination. In either case, employers favor the cheap labor, but workers of the dominant group, quite understandably, resist their employment with more or less racist anti-ethnic appeals. There are often bloody confrontations between the dominant workers and the ethnics as well as between the former and managers. In the long run the situation is stabilized by one or another of three devices: (1) The ethnics are driven out of the labor market by forced reimmigration. This strategy was used against Orientals on the U. S. West coast. (2) A caste system is established which relegates the ethnics to inferior jobs and allocates the better jobs to the dominant group. This strategy is widely used against women. (3) Wage differentials between the two groups are reduced so that managers again favor employing the dominant group. This third strategy is not mentioned by Bonacich, but it is frequently used by "liberal" work groups. For example, the male workers who have advocated equal pay for equal work regardless of sex have often done so to raise the cost of employing women in the hope of saving jobs for men.

Corporate power An advertisement for a book on the multi-national corporation asks, "Which institution will be around 100 years from now —France or General Motors?" This is a silly question perhaps, but if one compares the gross sales of the largest corporations with the gross product of the largest nations, General Motors and eight other corporations rank among the top fifty such "institutions." While corporate apologists paint the large corporations as harmless benefactors of mankind, critics accuse them of being producers of war, poverty, racism, and pollution. The most comprehensive analysis of the impact of corporate enterprise on other aspects of society is the collection of essays by Ivar Berg, *The Business of America.* This anthology would not satisfy apologists or critics for it does not provide a singular judgment *for* or *against* the large corporation. Instead, its fourteen essays are wide-ranging in their assessment of the impact of corporate enterprise. Topics range from the local community and United States international affairs to family, education, science, and the arts. One major topic not covered in Berg's 1968 anthology which would now seem deserving of extensive attention is the problem of pollution. More than any other single issue, the rising spectre of pollution has forced a systematic review of the relative benefits and costs of industrialization. It has impressed upon conservatives and radicals alike the need to get the process more nearly under human control.

Over the years one of the prime questions about industrialization has been the *control* of corporations. In the last century there were a number of colorful "captains of industry" or "robber barons," if you like. Their successors have not received the same sort of public notoriety and, in fact, it has been widely held in academic circles, at least since the 1930s, that effective control of corporations has moved into the hands of a class of salaried non-owning managers. This theory is expressed in naive form by Coleman (1973). The theory of bloodless "managerial revolution" has been seriously questioned by Zald (1969) and others. Villarejo (1961) has found that while most large corporations are "owned" by a multitude of small shareholders, in a goodly number of cases, the board of directors own enough stock to have effective operating control over the company. More recently, Levine (1972) has shown graphically just how closely interconnected the major United States corporations are. For example, General Motors, United States Steel, Ford, Chrysler, and General Electric are all connected by sharing one or more board members with the J. P. Morgan Bank of New York. Zeitlin (1970) has brought together a number of studies having to do both with the question of who controls the major corporations and also the potentially antisocial ends to which this power is being put. Carefully documented studies of this sort may well prove among the most intellectually engaging as well as socially important studies in the coming decade of industrial sociology.

THE INDUSTRIAL SOCIOLOGY YET TO COME

As noted at the outset, sociology arose in the nineteenth century out of the felt need for ways to understand and deal with the consequences of industrialization. Each successive stage of industrial sociology can be interpreted as a response to socially defined problems as well. The early community approach can be seen as an attempt to come to grips with those industrializing processes which were causing the eclipse of community. In like fashion, the factory approach can be seen as rising out of the mounting collective unrest of workers in the first half of the century. The cross-national comparative approach emerged after World War II when the United States was very much concerned with its new military, economic, and ideological role as one of the contending super-powers. Finally, the political economy approach which has just been reviewed emerged at a time when Americans have begun to look seriously at the differences between the quality of life promised and that currently realized in this era of super-productivity. Rather than predict what industrial sociology *will* become, I will finish this brief work by pointing to what I think industrial sociology *should* become to fulfill its historic role as a prime tool for coming to grips with the continuing industrial revolution.

No single theoretical orientation or a substantive focus should be paramount, although the family, community, and societal orientations and the six questions they address, will continue to be central. Specific researchers need to cover a wide range of topics, such as: the impact of women's increasing labor-force participation on industry and community, the dynamics of managerial careers in conglomerate corporations, the apparent convergence of communist and capitalist organizational forms and managerial ideologies, changing incentives to work, the impact of the military-industrial complex on industrial development and national policy, the disarticulation of education and employment, contemporary forms of entrepreneurship, the relationship between job careers and family careers, the effects of multi-national corporations on the domestic economies of small nations, the impact of super-productivity on societies whose structure has been predicated on scarcity, and the ideological uses of the ecology issue.

Whether investigating the link between technology and the moral order, discussing career contingencies with self-employed cab drivers, or tracing the link between the ideological content of pop music lyrics and the structure of the music industry, the researcher should satisfy four general directives:[5]

1. The particular research should be designed to give answers for larger questions.
2. These larger questions should include *both* the formulation and testing of social science theory *and* the definition and resolution of social policy issues.

---

5. While these four directives may seem "self-evident," the history of science cautions that researchers and whole disciplines may become mired in technical problem-solving or ideological confrontation that loses sight of the larger purposes of scientific inquiry (Kuhn, 1970). The social sciences, which so intimately touch human affairs, are particularly vulnerable as Gouldner (1970), Friedrichs (1970), Reynolds and Reynolds (1970), Oberschall (1972) and Ladner (1973) graphically illustrate.

3. Every available method of inquiry from case studies to computer simulation should be employed where appropriate to best illuminate the question at hand.
4. No belief, ideology, institution, or organization should be immune from close and dispassionate examination in the overall effort to bring the continuing process of industrialization more completely under human control.

References

Aiken, Michael, Louis A. Ferman, and Harold L. Sheppard
1968   Economic Failure, Alienation, and Extremism. Ann Arbor: University of Michigan Press.

Baran, Paul A. and Paul M. Sweezy
1966   Monopoly Capital, An Essay on the American Economic and Social Order. New York: Modern Reader.

Baritz, Loren
1960   The Servants of Power: A History of the Use of Social Science in American Industry. Middletown, Conn.: Wesleyan University Press.

Barnard, Chester
1938   The Functions of the Executive. Cambridge, Mass.: Harvard University Press.

Bendix, Reinhard
1956   Work and Authority in Industry. New York: John Wiley.

Bendix, Reinhard and Lloyd H. Fisher
1949   "The perspectives of Elton Mayo."
        Review of Economics and Statistics 31: 312–319.

Bennis, Warren G. and Philip Slater
1968   The Temporary Society. New York: Harper and Row.

Berg, Ivar
1971   Education and Jobs. Boston: Beacon Press.

Berg, Ivar, ed.
1968   The Business of America. New York: Harcourt, Brace & World.

Berger, Bennett M.
1960   Working-Class Suburb. Berkeley and Los Angeles: University of California Press.

Blau, Peter M.
1955   The Dynamics of Bureaucracy. Chicago: University of Chicago Press.

Blau, Peter M. and Otis Dudley Duncan
1967   The American Occupational Structure. New York: John Wiley.

Blauner, Robert
1964   Alienation and Freedom: The Factory Worker and His Industry. Chicago: University of Chicago Press.
1972   Racial Oppression in America. New York: Harper and Row.

Bonacich, Edna
1972   "A theory of ethnic antagonism: the split labor market." American Sociological Review 37 (October): 547–559.

Britt, David W. and Omer Galle
1972 "Industrial conflict and unionization." American Sociological Review 37 (February): 46–57.

Camp, Charles B.
1972 "Utopian GM plant in Ohio falls from grace under strain of balky machinery, workers." Wall Street Journal, January 31, p. 24.

Chandler, Margaret K.
1964 Management Rights and Union Interests. New York: McGraw-Hill.

Chinoy, Eli
1955 Automobile Workers and the American Dream. Garden City, N.Y.: Doubleday.

Coleman, James S.
1973 "Loss of power." American Sociological Review 38 (February): 1–17.

Denisoff, R. Serge and Richard A. Peterson, eds.
1972 *The Sounds of Social Change.* Chicago: Rand McNally.

Eisenstadt, S. N.
1964 "Breakdowns of modernization." Economic Development and Culture Change 12 (July): 345–367.
1966 Modernization: Protest and Change. Englewood Cliffs, N.J.: Prentice-Hall.

Ellul, Jacques
1964 The Technological Society. New York: Alfred A. Knopf.

Faunce, William A.
1968 Problems of an Industrial Society. New York: McGraw-Hill.

Frank, Andre Gunder
1972 "Sociology of development and the underdevelopment of sociology." Pages 321–397 in Dependence and Underdevelopment, ed. James D. Cockcroft, Andre Gunder Frank, and Dale L. Johnson. New York: Doubleday.

Friedrichs, Robert W.
1970 A Sociology of Sociology. New York: Free Press.

Galbraith, John Kenneth
1967 The New Industrial State. Boston: Houghton Mifflin.

Gouldner, Alvin W.
1952 "Red tape as a social problem." Pages 410–418 in Reader in Bureaucracy, ed. Robert K. Merton et al. New York: Free Press.
1954a Patterns of Industrial Bureaucracy. New York: Free Press.
1954b Wildcat Strike. Yellow Springs, Ohio: Antioch Press.
1970 The Coming Crisis of Western Sociology. New York: Basic Books.

Gusfield, Joseph
1963 Symbolic Crusade. Urbana: University of Illinois Press.

Harris, T. George
1973 "Work modules and the manhood pinch." Psychology Today, February, p. 32.

Howe, Irving, ed.
1972 The World of the Blue-Collar Worker. New York: Quadrangle.

Kuhn, Thomas S.
1970 The Structure of Scientific Revolutions. Chicago: University of Chicago Press.

Ladner, Joyce A., ed.
1973 The Death of White Sociology. New York: Random House.

Levine, Joel H.
1972 "The sphere of influence." American Sociological Review 37 (February): 14–27.

Lewis, Oscar
1966   La Vida. New York: Random House.

Lipset, Seymour Martin, Martin Trow, and James Coleman
1956   Union Democracy. New York: Free Press.

Lynd, Robert and Helen
1929   Middletown. New York: Harcourt, Brace.
1937   Middletown in Transition. New York: Harcourt, Brace.

Mantoux, Paul
1961   The Industrial Revolution in the Eighteenth Century: An Outline of the Beginnings of the Modern Factory System in England. New York: Harper and Row.

Martindale, Don
1960   The Nature and Types of Sociological Theory. Boston: Houghton Mifflin.

Mayo, Elton
1945   The Social Problems of an Industrial Civilization. Boston: Harvard University Press.

Mechanic, David
1962   "Sources of power of lower participants in complex organizations." Administrative Science Quarterly 7 (December): 349–364.

Merton, Robert K.
1968   Social Theory and Social Structure. New York: Free Press.

Mills, C. Wright
1951   White Collar: The American Middle Classes. New York: Oxford University Press.

Moore, Barrington, Jr.
1966   Social Origins of Dictatorship and Democracy: Lord and Peasant in the Making of the Modern World. Boston: Beacon Press.

Moore, Wilbert E.
1963   Social Change. Englewood Cliffs, N. J.: Prentice-Hall.

Moynihan, Daniel P.
1965   The Negro Family: The Case for National Action. U.S. Department of Labor: Washington, D.C.

Nisbet, Robert A.
1953   The Quest for Community. New York: Oxford University Press.
1966   The Sociological Tradition. New York: Basic Books.

Oberschall, Anthony
1973   Social Conflict and Social Movements. Englewood Cliffs, N.J.: Prentice-Hall.

Oberschall, Anthony, ed.
1972   The Establishment of Empirical Sociology. New York: Harper and Row.

Ogburn, William Fielding
1933   Social Change. New York: Viking Press.

Parsons, Talcott
1966   Societies: Evolutionary and Comparative Perspectives. Englewood Cliffs, N.J.: Prentice-Hall.
1964   "Evolutionary universals in society." American Sociological Review 29 (June): 339–357.

Perrow, Charles
1967   "A framework for the comparative analysis of organizations." American Sociological Review 32 (April): 194–208.
1972   Complex Organizations. Glenview, Ill.: Scott-Foresman.

Peterson, Richard A.
1973   The Industrial Order and Social Policy. Englewood Cliffs, N.J.: Prentice-Hall.

Peterson, Richard A. and David G. Berger
1971   "Entrepreneurship in organizations: evidence from the popular music industry." Administrative Science Quarterly 16 (March): 97–107.

Pope, Liston
1965   Millhands and Preachers. New Haven: Yale University Press.

Preston, Lee E.
1971   The Industry and Enterprise Structure of the U.S. Economy. New York: General Learning Press.

Reynolds, Larry T. and Janice M. Reynolds
1970   The Sociology of Sociology. New York: David McKay.

Riesman, David
1950   The Lonely Crowd. New Haven: Yale University Press.

Rostow, W. W.
1960   The Stages of Economic Growth: A Non-Communist Manifesto. New York: Cambridge University Press.

Seeman, Melvin
1959   "On the meaning of alienation." American Sociological Review 24 (December): 783–791.

Selznik, Philip
1949   TVA and the Grass Roots. Berkeley and Los Angeles: University of California Press.

Sheppard, Harold L. and Neal Q. Herrick
1972   Where Have All the Robots Gone? New York: Free Press.

Shostak, Arthur B.
1969   Blue-Collar Life. New York: Random House.

Simon, Herbert
1956   Models of Man. New York: Wiley.

Smelser, Neil J.
1959   Social Change in the Industrial Revolution. Chicago: University of Chicago Press.

Smith, Adam
1937   The Wealth of Nations. New York: Modern Library.

Stein, Maurice R.
1960   The Eclipse of Community. Princeton, New Jersey: Princeton University Press.

Stinchcombe, Arthur L.
1959   "Bureaucratic and craft administration of production: a comparative study." Administrative Science Quarterly 4 (September): 168–187.

Taylor, Frederick
1911   The Principles of Scientific Management. New York: Harper.

Thompson, James D.
1967   Organizations in Action: Social Science Bases of Administrative Theory. New York: McGraw-Hill.

Time
1973   "The new Stakhanovites." February 12, p. 73.

Van de Vall, Mark
1970   Labor Organizations. Cambridge: Cambridge University Press.

Villarejo, Don
1961   "Stock ownership and the control of corporations." Parts 1, 2 and 3. New University Thought (Autumn, Winter).

Walker, Charles R.
1957   Toward the Automatic Factory. New Haven: Yale University Press.
1962   Modern Technology and Civilization. New York: McGraw-Hill.

Westley, William A. and Margaret W.
1971   The Emerging Worker. Montreal: McGill University Press.

Wilhelm, Sidney M.
1970   Who Needs the Negro? Cambridge, Mass.: Shenkman.

Zald, Mayer N.
1969   "The power and functions of boards of directors: a theoretical synthesis." American Journal of Sociology 75 (July): 97–111.
1970   Organizational Change. Chicago: University of Chicago Press.

Zeitlin, Irving M.
1968   Ideology and the Development of Sociological Theory. Englewood Cliffs, N. J.: Prentice-Hall.

Zeitlin, Maurice, ed.
1970   American Society, Inc. Chicago: Markham.

Suggested Readings

This work has drawn heavily on a few books which are well worth reading in their own right. They include: Bendix (1956), Blauner (1964), Eisenstadt (1966), Gouldner (1954a), Lynd and Lynd (1929, 1936), Mills (1951), Perrow (1972), Peterson (1973), and Thompson (1967).

The *Wall Street Journal,* daily business-world newspaper, should be read both for information and for the perspective on the world of work which it presents.

Four quite different anthologies provide convenient collections of valuable articles: William A. Faunce offers a set of articles on the range of factory sociology topics (*Readings in Industrial Sociology,* N.Y.: Appleton-Century-Crofts, 1967). Arthur B. Shostak and William Gomburg relate the world of work to the blue collar community in their anthology (*Blue Collar World,* Englewood Cliffs, N.J.: Prentice-Hall, 1964). The articles in Berg (1968) show many links between corporate enterprise and the range of topics covered in the community section. In his case book, S. Prakash Sethi details a number of situations which show the influences of business corporations on societal issues ranging from public health to international politics (*Up Against the Corporate Wall,* Englewood Cliffs, N.J.: Prentice-Hall, 1971).

The dynamics of industrial society are perhaps best seen in the carefully researched analyses of one or another aspect of the process. The following are suggested because they deal with vital questions, illustrate different methodologies, and make good reading. The list is not comprehensive; rather it is intended as a sampler for the interested student:

Eric William (*Capitalism and Slavery,* N.Y.: Capricorn Books, 1966) presents a careful historical analysis of the great contribution that the African slave trade made to the early development of industrialization.

Using sophisticated computer-dependent techniques, Blau and Duncan (1967), trace the relationship between social background, education, occupation, and social class mobility.

Hollywood Studio Musicians (Chicago: Aldine, 1971) by Robert Faulkner, provides a detailed portrayal based on participant observation of the career contingencies of workers whose artistry is constantly constrained by technological, organizational, and market demands beyond their control.

Employing the investigative techniques of political science, Robert Engler unfolds numerous complex links between large organizations and governments around the world in his analysis of *The Politics of Oil* (Chicago: Univ. of Chicago Press 1961).

Utilizing a questionnaire survey, Sheppard and Herrick (1972) assay the current high levels of alienation and discontent among American workers, young and old. Aiken et al. (1968) use the community study technique to trace the impact of a factory closing on workers, their families, and their town.

Finally, in a study which uses most of the methods mentioned above, Joan London and Henry Anderson analyze the bitter struggles over migratory workers' rights, ethnic identity, and union organization in the California agriculture industry (*So Shall Ye Reap.* New York: Crowell, 1971).

THE BOBBS-MERRILL REPRINT SERIES

The author recommends for supplementary reading the following related material. Please fill out this form and mail.

Indicate number of reprints desired

___ **Baratz, Morton** 1956 "Corporate Giants and the Power Structure." Western Political Quarterly, pp. 406-415.   **PS-13**/66501   40¢

___ **Bendix, Reinhard** 1959 "Industrialization, Ideologies, and Social Structure." American Sociological Review, pp. 613-623.
     S-17/66426   40¢

___ **Carey, Alex** 1967 "The Hawthorne Studies: A Radical Criticism." American Sociological Review, pp. 403-416.   **S-557**/66934   40¢

___ **Chandler, Alfred D., Jr.** 1959 "The Beginnings of 'Big Business' in American Industry." Business History Review, pp. 1-31.
     H-35/64889   40¢

___ **Chinoy, Eli** 1952 "The Tradition of Opportunity and the Aspirations of Automobile Workers." American Journal of Sociology, pp. 453-459.
     S-41/66447   40¢

___ **Cottrell, W. F.** 1951 "Death by Dieselization: A Case Study in the Reaction to Technological Change." American Sociological Review, pp. 358-365.   **S-53**/66459   40¢

___ **Cyert, R. M. and J. G. March** 1963 "A Summary of Basic Concepts in the Behavioral Theory of the Firm." Pp. 114-127 in A Behavioral Theory of the Firm, ed. Cyert and March. Prentice-Hall.
     Econ-78/68177   40¢

___ **Gellner, Ernest** 1967 "Democracy and Industrialisation." European Journal of Sociology, pp. 47-70.   **S-697**/68715   60¢

___ **Goldthorpe, John H.** 1964 "Social Stratification in Industrial Society." Pp. 97–122 in Sociological Review Monograph #8, The Development of Industrial Society, ed. Paul Halmos.   **S-585**/66962   40¢

___ **Homan, George C.** 1951 "The Western Electric Researches." Pp. 210–241 in Human Factors in Management, Rev. Ed., ed. Schuyler Dean Hoslett. Harper and Bros.   **S-123**/66526   40¢

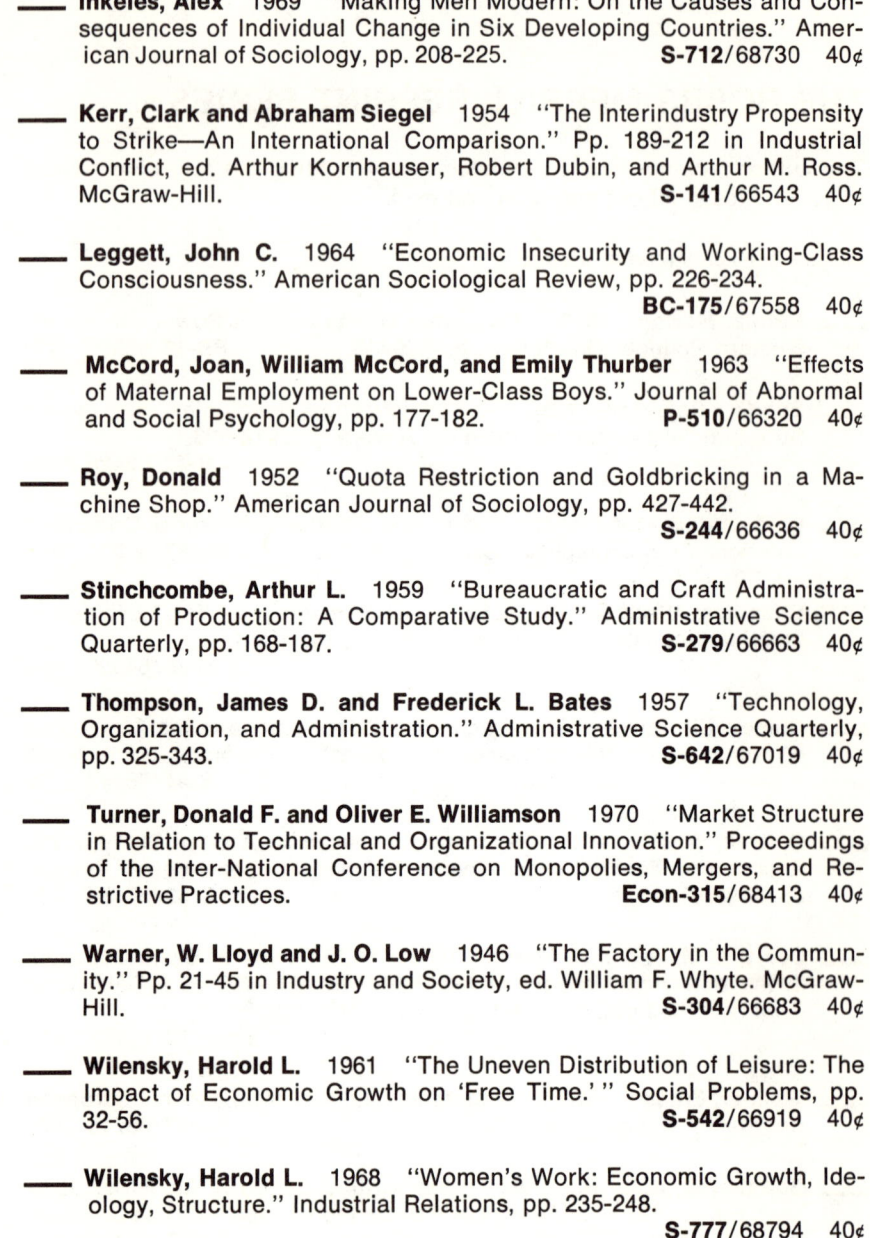

_____ **Inkeles, Alex** 1969 "Making Men Modern: On the Causes and Consequences of Individual Change in Six Developing Countries." American Journal of Sociology, pp. 208-225. **S-712**/68730 40¢

_____ **Kerr, Clark and Abraham Siegel** 1954 "The Interindustry Propensity to Strike—An International Comparison." Pp. 189-212 in Industrial Conflict, ed. Arthur Kornhauser, Robert Dubin, and Arthur M. Ross. McGraw-Hill. **S-141**/66543 40¢

_____ **Leggett, John C.** 1964 "Economic Insecurity and Working-Class Consciousness." American Sociological Review, pp. 226-234. **BC-175**/67558 40¢

_____ **McCord, Joan, William McCord, and Emily Thurber** 1963 "Effects of Maternal Employment on Lower-Class Boys." Journal of Abnormal and Social Psychology, pp. 177-182. **P-510**/66320 40¢

_____ **Roy, Donald** 1952 "Quota Restriction and Goldbricking in a Machine Shop." American Journal of Sociology, pp. 427-442. **S-244**/66636 40¢

_____ **Stinchcombe, Arthur L.** 1959 "Bureaucratic and Craft Administration of Production: A Comparative Study." Administrative Science Quarterly, pp. 168-187. **S-279**/66663 40¢

_____ **Thompson, James D. and Frederick L. Bates** 1957 "Technology, Organization, and Administration." Administrative Science Quarterly, pp. 325-343. **S-642**/67019 40¢

_____ **Turner, Donald F. and Oliver E. Williamson** 1970 "Market Structure in Relation to Technical and Organizational Innovation." Proceedings of the Inter-National Conference on Monopolies, Mergers, and Restrictive Practices. **Econ-315**/68413 40¢

_____ **Warner, W. Lloyd and J. O. Low** 1946 "The Factory in the Community." Pp. 21-45 in Industry and Society, ed. William F. Whyte. McGraw-Hill. **S-304**/66683 40¢

_____ **Wilensky, Harold L.** 1961 "The Uneven Distribution of Leisure: The Impact of Economic Growth on 'Free Time.'" Social Problems, pp. 32-56. **S-542**/66919 40¢

_____ **Wilensky, Harold L.** 1968 "Women's Work: Economic Growth, Ideology, Structure." Industrial Relations, pp. 235-248. **S-777**/68794 40¢

The Bobbs-Merrill Company, Inc.
College Division
4300 West 62nd Street
Indianapolis, Indiana 46268

Instructors ordering for class use will receive *upon request* a complimentary desk copy of each title ordered in quantities of 10 or more. Refer to author and *complete* letter-number code when ordering reprints.

☐ Payment enclosed   ☐ Bill me (on orders for $5 or more only)

_____ Course number   _____ Expected enrollment

☐ For examination   ☐ Desk copy

Bill To_____

ADDRESS_____

CITY_____STATE_____ZIP_____

Ship To_____

ADDRESS_____

CITY_____STATE_____ZIP_____

Please send me _____ copies of the sociology reprint catalog.

Please send me related reprints catalogs in_____

_____

Any reseller is free to charge whatever price he wishes for our books.

For your convenience please use complete form when placing your order.